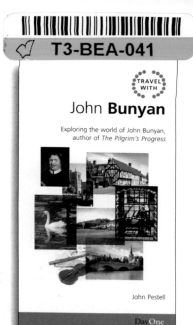

TRAVEL
WITH

John **Bunyan**

Exploring the world of John Bunyan,
author of *The Pilgrim's Progress*

John Pestell

Day One

Series Editor: Brian H Edwards

Day One

John **Bunyan**

❷ A cottage home in Elstow

Newly released from the parliamentary army, the wild, careless and penniless soldier moved into a home in Elstow with his young bride. The white, half-timbered cottages, with their overhanging storeys and gabled porches, are still much as Bunyan would have known them. To step into the parish church and churchyard is to step back into the seventeenth century

When Bunyan returned to the area in 1647 following his time in the army he quickly resumed his civilian life. At this time he appears to have been as careless as before, because he wrote, 'Here ... were judgements and mercy, but neither of them did awaken my soul to righteousness; wherefore I sinned still, and grew more and more rebellious against God, and careless of mine own salvation.'

According to descriptions he was quite tall with fair, reddish hair, a ruddy complexion and a quick wit. Such a lad soon found a wife and in 1649, at twenty one

Above: Picturesque cottages in the village of Elstow—referred to as Elnestou in the Domesday Book

Opposite: 'The Swan,' Elstow High Street. In Bunyan's time this was a stopping off point for the London–Bedford stage coach

❻ The pen in the prison

Offered the choice of ending his preaching or remaining in prison, Bunyan chose to stay where he was, and so began his most valuable ministry of writing. *The Pilgrim's Progress* was created in the cold gloom of a town lock-up, the buildings and sites in it inspired by places in Bedford that Bunyan knew and loved

John never wasted time! As well as making bootlaces to bring in a little money for his family and speaking to fellow prisoners and parishioners regarding the Christian faith, he would sit in his cell and write. For a number of years before his imprisonment, he had been responsible for several short tracts, but between 1660 to 1666 he issued nine different publications including, in 1664, *One Thing is Needful*, which was published on a single sheet and distributed by his wife and family in order to help them financially. In all, over sixty works ranging from one-page essays to masterful volumes, along with verses and rhyme were to come from Bunyan's pen during his life.

Bunyan had published his first article back in 1656, soon after his conversion. This was in response to a visit to Bedfordshire during 1654 of William Dewsbury, a national leader of the Quakers. Dewsbury had aroused interest in the religious group but Bunyan and other Puritans at that time considered their beliefs unscriptural. Bunyan condemned the group as heretical and entitled

his article *Some Gospel truths opened,* according to the Scriptures, of the Divine and Human Nature of Jesus Christ ... Published for the good of God's chosen ones, by that unworthy servant of Christ, John Bunyan of Bedford, by the grace of God, preacher of the Gospel of His Dear Son. This extraordinarily long and ungainly title was a practice that the Puritans used in order to present their readers with a broad outline of the contents in the book. It was 216 pages long and showed what an outstanding knowledge of the Bible Bunyan already possessed. The publisher, Matthais Cowley, was a bookseller in Newport Pagnell, an acquaintance from the time that

Opposite: John Bunyan in Prison. A stained glass window in Bunyan Meeting Free church, Bedford. Commemorating the tercentenary of the publication of 'The Pilgrim's Progress' in February 1978

CONTENTS

© Day One Publications 2002 First printed 2002 Reprinted 2005

All Scripture quotations are taken from The Authorized Version

A Catalogue record is held at The British Library   ISBN 1 903087 12

Published by Day One Publications Ryelands Road, Leominster, HR6 8NZ

☎ 01568 613 740 FAX 01568 611 473 email—sales@dayone.co.uk www.dayone.co.uk All rights reserved

Design and Art Direction: Steve Devane   Printed by Gutenberg, Malta

Dedication: Peter Charles Pestell— A dear father and an admirer of John Bunyan's life, history and works

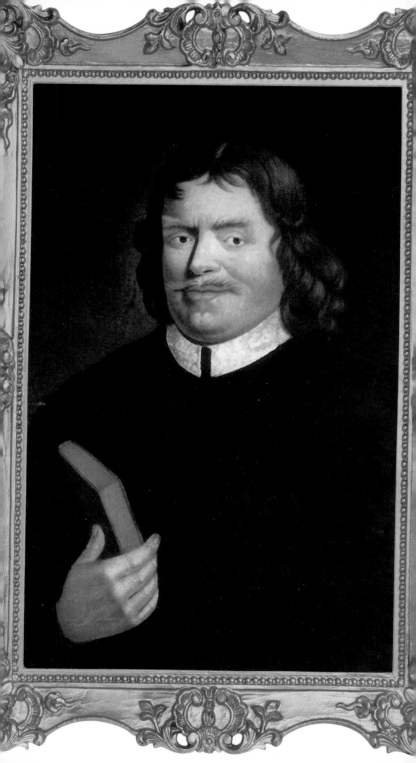

Meet John Bunyan

'John, there's a warrant out for your arrest, you know! Perhaps we should cancel the meeting?' The defiant preacher responded, 'We need not be ashamed to preach—it is God's word!' There was a hush as John Bunyan commenced to pray, but hardly had he begun when, without warning, the village constable burst into the room of the isolated farmhouse. The gathering was thrown into confusion and many of the hearers became alarmed and fearful of what would happen next. Calmly the tall, red-haired preacher spoke a few words of encouragement to his small country congregation before being led away.

John Bunyan was under arrest for daring to preach the gospel in a Bedfordshire village!

During the middle years of the 17th century, England saw many who made a stand for freedom of conscience to worship outside of the Church of England. Following the civil war that had divided the nation for nine long years, they were imprisoned without a proper trial or hearing for their faith and conviction as the new monarch, Charles II, peevishly tried to restore the rule of law across the realm.

John Bunyan was arrested and sent to prison for preaching without a licence from the Church of England. He would spend the next twelve years in Bedford Gaol because of his beliefs.

Born into a poor Bedfordshire family, Bunyan grew up as an idle lad, known locally for his lying and cursing; yet he was to become a world famous figure even in his own lifetime. Though barely literate, he would eventually pen what is still today probably one of the best-known classic titles ever to be written—*The Pilgrim's Progress*.

Many have written on the life, times and theology of this 17th century writer, preacher, and prisoner of faith and conscience. This book presents the story of Bunyan together with tourist details and information connected with Bedfordshire's famous son, who became widely known as 'the tinker from Elstow'.

Pictured: John Bunyan. From a copy of a portrait in the National Portrait Gallery, London, by Thomas Sadler

A map of Bunyan highlights

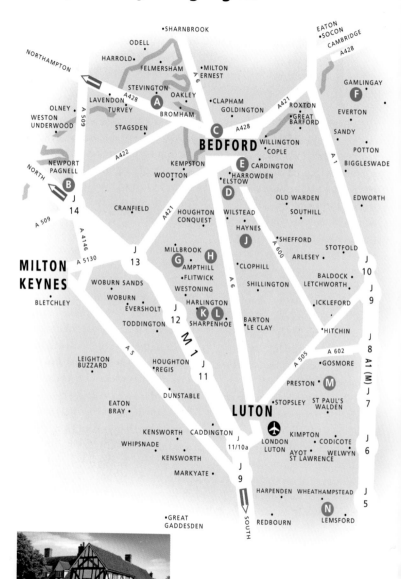

Elstow—see map reference 'D'

Key to map opposite

A Stevington Village

The Cross and Church Well may have been in

Bunyan's mind when writing *The Pilgrim's Progress*.

B Newport Pagnell

Bunyan was garrisoned here as a soldier during the Civil War, 1644-47.

C Bedford

The county town where Bunyan lived from 1655 and was imprisoned for twelve years from 1660. The church he founded stands in the town; adjacent is the Bunyan museum. A statue dedicated to him stands at the north end of the High Street.

D Elstow

The village where Bunyan attended the parish church during his childhood, adjacent to the green where he famously played tip-cat. Nearby is the site of his cottage where he lived during his first marriage. The Moot Hall on the green is now a museum of seventeenth century rural life.

E Harrowden

The tiny hamlet where Bunyan was born in 1628.

F Gamlingay

The independent church at Bedford set up a church in the village and often met here during times of harassment.

G Millbrook

The village gorge is thought to be the inspiration for the Valley of the Shadow of Death in *The Pilgrim's Progress*.

H Houghton House and Hill Difficulty

Just north of Ampthill, these sites are thought to have been depicted by Bunyan in *The Pilgrim's Progress*.

I Haynes

Mid-Bedfordshire village where the Bedford Baptists often met in secret and Bunyan preached. In the church minute book of the time it is spelt Hawnes.

K Harlington

The Manor House, in which he was interrogated, stands on the crossroads at the heart of the village. The parish church contains a 'Bunyan' stained glass and the altar table was made from an oak tree that Bunyan used as a natural pulpit in a nearby field.

L Lower Sampsell

Bunyan was arrested in November 1660 at a farm in this hamlet. The building no longer stands today.

M Wainwood, Preston

Site of a natural amphitheatre in woodland where Bunyan often preached in secret.

N Coleman Green, Wheathampstead

The remains of a cottage reputed to be that in which Bunyan would lodge whilst travelling between his home and London. The nearby public house bears his name.

1   Tinker, soldier, poor man?

A plaque in a cornfield is an unusual memorial to a man who was born in poverty, despised as the village hooligan and began his working life mending pots and pans. However, this man was to write one of the best known books of all time and to become one of the most popular preachers of his generation

Looking south across the fields from the busy, modern Bedford by-pass, it is hard to imagine the same scene nearly four hundred years ago. True, there is still the tiny hamlet of Harrowden nestling in the low hillside, below the two imposing giant hangars that now dominate the horizon—a legacy of Great Britain's airship industry and the departure point of the ill-fated R101, that crashed in Northern France whilst on its maiden flight to India in October 1930. Yet, were it not for a plaque on a large slab of stone, half a mile to the

Above: A thatched cottage in Harrowden near to the site of John Bunyan's birthplace

Opposite: Arable farming still has a strong visible presence within the landscape of England's Bedfordshire

Top: Drawing of Bunyan's birthplace at Harrowden (demolished in the 19th century). Taken from an old print

Above: The doomed R 101 airship, born at Cardington in 1930, seen in a rare photograph

west of Harrowden, in the corner of a cornfield, the site and memory of John Bunyan's birthplace would have vanished long ago.

John Bunyan was born in the late Summer to Autumn of 1628, and was christened on 30 November 1628, three years after Charles I had succeeded to the throne. At that time England had become professedly Protestant through the long reign of Elizabeth and that of her successor James I. However, this position was continually threatened.

Bunyan's parents, Thomas and Margaret, were married in Elstow Abbey Church on 23 May 1627. Thomas's first wife, Anne, had died, childless, earlier that same year, after five years of marriage. Thomas and his new wife set up their home in a cottage at Harrowden, a mile south east of Elstow village. The family had been connected with the area for many years. In fact, at one time it was known locally as '*Bonyon's End*'. As early as 1327 a '*William Bonyun*' lived at Harrowden, and records show that in 1199 a '*William Buniun*' rented land from the Abbess of Elstow at Wilshamstead (Wilstead), 3.5 kilometres (2 miles) south of Harrowden on the London road. The surname 'Bunyan' was spelt variously over the generations and historical records show over thirty different variations. John's father was recorded by the vicar at Elstow when he was registered at birth in 1603 as 'Bonnionn'.

Thomas was a tinker or tinsmith by profession—a mender

of pots and pans. It was this simple trade which his son John was to take up for himself. In his autobiographical book, *Grace Abounding*, John Bunyan relates of his family, 'My descent then, was as is well known by many, of a low and inconsiderable generation; my ancestors being of the meanest and most despised of all families in the land.' He continues affectionately, 'Wherefore I have not here, as others, to boast of noble blood, or of a high-born state, according to the flesh; though, all things considered, I magnify the heavenly Majesty, for that by this door He brought me into this world, to partake of the grace and life that is in Christ by the gospel.'

Boyhood

Very little is known of the early years of John Bunyan's life. A sister, Margaret, was born in 1630 and his younger brother, William, three years later. John was grateful for his education, of which he wrote, 'It pleased God to put it into their hearts [his parents] to put me to school, to learn both to read and write; the which I also attained, according to the rate of other poor men's children; though, to my shame I confess, I did soon lose that little I learned.' Where he actually went to school and for how long is uncertain. Suggestions differ between the former Harpur Grammar School in Bedford, and a village school at Houghton Conquest, three to four miles south west of Elstow on the road to Ampthill. The county town boasts four Harpur Trust schools today. However, the sites

Top: Erected in the year of the Festival of Britain, this stone marks the place of Bunyan's birth

Above: *The Norman font in Elstow church where Bunyan was christened in 1628*

Opposite and below:
River life; The River
Great Ouse, Bedford
plays host to a variety
of wildlife

Bottom: Elstow
Brook. Bunyan and his
family would cross the
brook near this point
as they walked a mile
across the fields
to Elstow village and
the church from
their home

of the two schools mentioned here are unclear. Bunyan may even have received a simple one-to-one tutorial education in the local neighbourhood. Wherever the schooling took place, he admits that it had little impact on him.

By the time he was nine or ten John was living a reckless life. In later years he wrote, 'I had but few equals for cursing, swearing, lying and blaspheming the holy name of God ... I became so settled and rooted in these things that they became a sort of second nature to me.' His conscience pricked him many times as he sat in Elstow church listening to Puritan preaching. John was immensely troubled with thoughts of God's judgements and his own danger of ending up in hell. 'These things, I say, when I was but a child but nine or ten years old, did so distress my soul, that when in the midst of my many sports and childish vanities, amidst my vain companions, I was often much cast down and afflicted

in my mind therewith, yet could I not let go my sins.' He wished at this time that God would leave him alone because, he records, I 'desire not the knowledge of thy ways' (Job 21:14 AV).

Throughout his childhood and early life, Bunyan tells us that; 'God did not utterly leave me, but followed me still, not now with convictions, but judgments; yet, such as were mixed with mercy. For once I fell into a creek of the sea, and hardly escaped drowning. Another time I fell out of a boat into Bedford river, but mercy yet preserved me alive. Besides, another time, being in the field with one of my companions, it chanced that an adder passed over the highway; so I, having a stick in my hand, struck her over the back; and having stunned her, I forced open her mouth with my stick, and plucked her sting out with my fingers, by which act, had not God been merciful, I might, by my desperateness, have brought myself to mine end.'

In 1644 during an influenza epidemic John's mother died, followed a month later by his fourteen year old sister, Margaret. This greatly distressed John. The pain was to turn quickly into anger and bitterness when, in March that same year, his father hastily married for the third time.

A Parliamentary soldier

About that time there was a demand locally for military recruits. Local villages were scouted for sturdy young men, and John Bunyan, now carefree and careless—'without God in the world'—and without regard to his father, left the family home in the late summer of 1644. Having barely reached the required age of sixteen he signed up as a soldier in Oliver Cromwell's Parliamentary and largely 'Puritan' army to fight in the Civil War against the King's men.

John Bunyan was billeted at Newport Pagnell, a small market town 20 kilometres (13 miles) to the west of Bedford, just over the Buckinghamshire border. Today, the town lies on the very north-eastern edge of the new city of Milton Keynes. The name Newport means 'New Market Town', while Pagnell derives from the Paganell family who had a castle there on the site which is now, appropriately, Castle Close. Local archaeological finds suggest that there were settlements here throughout the Iron Age and the Roman occupation. It is probably inevitable that a settlement should be built at this junction of two rivers, the Great Ouse and the Lovat. In the late 10th century, a Royal Mint was established and the town became an important administrative centre for North Buckinghamshire. At one time

Newport Pagnell was at the centre of the local lace industry. At the eastern end of the town, at the top of the hill, stands the Church of St. Peter and St. Paul, which overlooks the tranquil meadows bordering the River Lovat. The area around the church retains much of the quality of a fortified town. It is probably in this church that Bunyan would have sat and heard long sermons each Sunday during his army period in the town from 1644–1647, as all soldiers were expected to attend divine worship. Each soldier was given a pocket Bible, first issued in 1643. Inside the cover were comments particular to the military such as 'A Soldier must

The Puritans and Civil War

The Puritans were originally named because of their efforts to purify the Church of England during the reign of Queen Elizabeth (1558-1603). Puritans were not prepared to compromise the Scriptures in the worship of God, and tried to conform the national church to the Bible in its government, worship and practices.

In 1559 Parliament passed the Act of Supremacy declaring that Elizabeth 1 was the Supreme Governor of the church in all spiritual and ecclesiastical issues. Elizabeth sought to enforce the legislation vigorously. The Act of Uniformity, issued the same year, imposed severe penalties on any cleric and preacher who deviated from the Prayer Book order of service, used by the Church of England. Those who deliberately abstained from parish church services were punished. John Bunyan was

to feel the full power of this law in 1660.

During the early 1600s some Puritans who had despaired of any change in England, crossed to Holland to escape persecution and began to practise their beliefs on the continent. This separatist movement developed when a group from Holland and England, later known as 'The Pilgrim Fathers', sailed from Plymouth in September 1620, on the 'Mayflower' for America, and began a new life in Massachusetts, New England.

When James I came to the throne there had been hope that religious reform would progress. However, the struggle intensified and

cry unto his God in his heart in the very instant of battle' and 'A Soldier must not do wickedly'.

When Bunyan first arrived in Newport Pagnell, the minister at St. Peter and St. Paul's was a Samuel Austin. However, during 1646 he was removed from his position by Sir Samuel Luke of Cople, Bedfordshire, the governor of the town's garrison, as he was not congenial to the Parliamentary regiment. Records show that the following year a young Puritan cleric, John Gibbs of St. Mary's, Bedford, succeeded him. Gibbs, who was eighteen months older than Bunyan, eventually became a life-long friend of the Bedfordshire tinker. He too was ejected from the

Above: Springtime along the River Ouse brings some spectacular floral displays

failed to improve even when Charles I succeeded him to the throne in 1625. The King and Parliament became locked in a struggle to determine who, ultimately, ruled England. A civil war between the King's 'Royalists' or 'Cavaliers' on the one side and the Parliamentarians or 'Roundheads' on the other erupted in 1642, mainly because of the strong differences and religious tensions in the national church and the King's belief in absolute right to rule. The Parliamentarians, under the leadership of Oliver Cromwell, dealt a series of defeats to the Royalists over seven years of fighting throughout the country. It

may be that Bunyan's regiment, based at Newport Pagnell, was involved in one of the decisive battles against the King in 1645 at Naseby, only fifteen miles north of their garrison. The civil disorder only ended when Charles was arrested, tried for treason and eventually executed in January 1649.

Oliver Cromwell became the Lord Protector in place of the King in 1653. Following his death in 1658, his son Richard proved an unsuitable replacement and the nation restored the monarchy when Charles II came to the throne in 1660. The struggle in the Church was renewed when an Act of Parliament was passed

which required conformity to rules which the Puritans were simply unable to follow. In 1662 over two thousand ministers and leaders in the Church of England left their churches.

The Puritans were known for the purity of life that they led. Hard work, self-discipline and piety became their hallmark. Blasphemy, drunkenness, immoral behaviour, gambling, corrupt business practice and participation in theatrical performances were all forbidden. Some historians suggest the Puritan period came to an end in 1662 although their beliefs and attitudes continued to influence society.

parish church in 1660 and began independent meetings in a secluded barn in the centre of Newport Pagnell. Today, the United Reformed church, set back behind 73, High Street, stands on the same site.

The road south from the town centre (St. John Street) crosses the River Lovat at Tickford Bridge. Built in 1810, it is the oldest cast iron bridge in Britain still carrying traffic on a daily basis. Just 200 metres further on from the bridge is the first home of one of the most famous and exclusive names in motoring—Aston Martin-Lagonda, whose cars were produced here from 1964.

There is no known legacy to Bunyan in the town but his period in the army is documented in various accounts, although the majority of these appear to be speculative. The fact that he himself speaks little of his army days may lead us to conclude that it was a time he wished to forget rather than divulge, apart from

God's overruling mercy in preserving his life. In '*Grace Abounding*' Bunyan recalls one significant event from this period with a note of thankfulness: 'When I was a soldier, I, with others, were drawn out to go to such a place to besiege it; but when I was just ready to go, one of the company [nothing is known of this army companion] desired to go in my room; to which, when I had consented, he took my place; and coming to the siege, as he stood sentinel, he was shot into the head with a musket bullet, and died.' Bunyan was to later write of God's judgements and mercy, neither of which changed his attitude at the time. On the contrary, he grew more rebellious and careless about his soul's salvation and faith in God.

Sometime during 1647 Bunyan left the army and returned to his native Elstow and to the life of a tinker. He had left his family home as a boisterous youth but returned as a careless man looking for a wife.

Oliver Cromwell

Oliver Cromwell was born on 25 April 1599 in Huntingdon, twenty miles east north east of Bedford. He was educated at Huntingdon Grammar School, now the Cromwell museum, followed by a year at Sidney Sussex College, Cambridge, known for its Puritan bias, which influenced his life.

Cromwell studied at the Inns Court in London where he met and married his wife, Elizabeth, in 1620. They were devoted to each other throughout their long marriage and had eight children - four boys and four girls. After their marriage the Cromwell family lived on a farm in St Ives, Cambridgeshire. In 1636 he inherited a large estate from a maternal uncle, in Ely. His inheritance also brought him the

position of a local tax collector. It made him into a man of property and gave him considerable local status in the area.

Until 1640 Cromwell paid

Above: Tickford Bridge (1810), Newport Pagnell today with the church in the background. Bunyan worshipped here during his time in the army between 1644–1647

no significant role in national affairs. At that time England was in religious and political turmoil. When the Civil War eventually broke out in the summer of 1642 Cromwell was an officer in the Parliamentary army. Over the next few years he was quickly promoted following several notable successes against the King's army until he became a lieutenant general. This was a remarkable achievement for a man who probably had no military experience before 1642. Cromwell consistently attributed his military success to God's will. His personal courage and skill, his care in training and equipping his men and the tight discipline he imposed both on and off the battlefield were also factors that made Oliver Cromwell such a great leader. He rose from modest beginnings to become one of the most powerful men in the nation as head of the state, the 'Lord Protector', following the execution of Charles I in early 1649. Oliver Cromwell died in 1658.

Cromwell Web site:
www.olivercromwell.org

Pictured: The statue to Oliver Cromwell at St. Ives, Cambs, erected in 1901

Olney

The small picturesque market town of Olney lies six miles north of Newport Pagnell at the very tip of north Buckinghamshire, in the Ouse Valley. Olney was recorded in the Domesday Survey of 1086 as Olnei and the unusually wide High Street remains much as it was in the 17th and 18th centuries. About 60 buildings are listed as of historic or architectural interest, and many are constructed from local limestone so that areas of the town resemble parts of the Cotswolds.

The 14th century Church of St. Peter and St. Paul, whose spire is a well known and much loved local landmark, dominates the southern part of the town. It was here that John Newton, a converted slave trader now best known as a composer of hymns, was the curate between 1764–1779. Newton's friend and neighbour was the poet William Cowper (pronounced 'Cooper'), who wrote the comic ballad John Gilpin, and together they published the *Olney Hymns* (1779), the most famous of which are 'Amazing Grace' and, 'God moves in a mysterious way.' John Newton is buried in the churchyard at Olney and his tombstone is visible. The Cowper and Newton Museum occupies the house in Market Square that was once Cowper's home and celebrates their lives. Olney was once a centre for a thriving lace

Right: The summer house in William Cowper's garden where he with John Newton and William Bull would sit.Olney parish church is in the background

Below: John Newton

Bottom: Well worth a visit: The Cowper & Newton Museum, Orchard Side, Market Square, Olney. Check our travel guide on page 22 for full details of opening times

industry, and examples of local work can also be found in the Museum as well as displays of fine archaeological specimens that were found locally.

Reference is also made in the museum to William Bull who was sent out to preach from the Bunyan Meeting, Bedford. He became the minister of the Independents in Newport Pagnell in 1764 and founded an academy for would-be preachers there in 1782. The old manse building Bull used for his evangelical students still stands in the centre of the town at 73, High Street, (near a pelican crossing). The United Reformed church, set back through the archway to the left, is built on the site of an ancient meeting barn used by John Bunyan's friend, John Gibbs, founder of the Independent church in Newport Pagnell in 1660.

When John Newton left Olney for a London parish, he introduced his friend William Bull to Cowper. They enjoyed each other's company and soon Bull was a regular visitor to Cowper's home.

Writing on one occasion to a friend, Cowper described Bull: 'A Dissenter, but a Liberal one; a man of letters and of genius, a master of fine imagination .... He can be lively without levity, and pensive without objection. Such a man is Mr. Bull. But he smokes tobacco! Nothing is perfect.'

TRAVEL INFORMATION

Harrowden

Site of Bunyan's birth place

OS Grid reference TL 064473

By car: (10 minutes drive). From Bedford town centre travelling south via London Road (A600) towards Shefford and Hitchin. Cross the Bedford southern bypass after approximately 3.5 kilometres (2 miles) (A421) and after quarter of a mile turn right at next crossroads into Harrowden. At the end of the road there is a farm on the left and a bridleway to the right towards Bedford.

Above: 73 High Street, Newport Pagnell, the home of William Bull circa 1764

Car parking is difficult here—please do not block farm gateways. Continue on foot taking the bridleway to the right of a sign marked 'Bunyan's Farm'. After crossing a stream (approx 200 metres) turn left in a field with the stream on your left. (Here there is a sign giving details of Bunyan's birthplace). The cottage was demolished during the early 19th century, however, a small oak beam exhibited in the Bunyan Museum, Bedford, is reputed to be part of the structure, and there are also two large cottage keys on display. The granite memorial stone, erected during the Festival of Britain in 1951 at the site of Bunyan's birthplace, is in the near left-hand corner of the next field beyond the wooden perimeter fence.

Alternatively: To view the site from the road: At the intersection of the A421/A 600, turn west onto the A421 towards Milton Keynes. After half a mile there is a parking lay-by on the left. The stone marking the site of Bunyan's birthplace can be seen in the far left-hand corner of the field immediately behind the trees that are by this parking area.

(Note: In summertime it may not be possible to see the stone if crops are growing in the field.)

By Public Transport:
☎ 0870 608 2 608 for timetable and fare information.

Bus service No117, Clapham to Wilstead, from Bedford town centre bus station, passes Harrowden crossroads. Alight from the bus here, then walk through Harrowden as detailed above to the birthplace site, approximately 1.5 kilometres (1mile).

Bus service No 106/107, Bedford rail station to Harrowden Road, travels from the town centre to Harrowden Road. Alight from the bus here then walk via Harrowden Lane (a footpath opposite Christ the King church), past the fish and chip shop to cross Winchester Road and Meadowsweet Drive. Enter the bridleway to the left of Foxglove Way. Continue through the housing estate and under the A421 Bedford bypass via the subway. After approx 1000 metres is a stream. On the right there is a sign giving details to the site of Bunyan's birthplace in the field beyond.

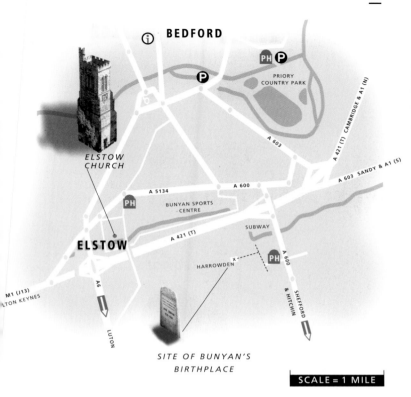

SITE OF BUNYAN'S BIRTHPLACE

SCALE = 1 MILE

Newport Pagnell

OS Grid reference SP 915450

By car: From Bedford town centre take the A428 west towards Northampton, then at Bromham turn on to the A422 to Newport Pagnell. From the M1 Motorway Go to Junction 14, A509 north. Newport Pagnell is 3.5 kilometres (2 miles). There is a town centre car park or street parking is an alternative where appropriate.

By Public Transport: Bedford town centre bus station Service 132 to Milton Keynes via Newport Pagnell. Travel line information ☎ 0870 608 2 608

A town map is available from Newport Pagnell Town Council on ☎ 01908 618756 or the Tourist Information Centre, ☎ 01908 232525

Olney

OS Grid reference SP 915505

By car: Olney is ten kilometres (6 miles) north of Newport Pagnell on the A509. There is ample parking in the town centre and on the market square (not Thursdays).

By Public Transport: Bus service X2 Bedford to Northampton service travels via Olney at regular times Monday to Saturday. Travel line information, ☎ 0870 608 2 608.

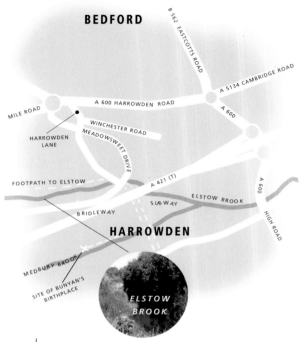

BEDFORD

B 562 EASTCOTTS ROAD

A 5134 CAMBRIDGE ROAD

A 600 HARROWDEN ROAD

A 600

MILE ROAD

WINCHESTER ROAD

HARROWDEN LANE

MEADOWSWEET DRIVE

FOOTPATH TO ELSTOW

A 421 (T)

ELSTOW BROOK

SUBWAY

A 600

HIGH ROAD

BRIDLEWAY

HARROWDEN

MEDBURY BROOK

SITE OF BUNYAN'S BIRTHPLACE

ELSTOW BROOK

SCALE = 1/2 MILE

Above: *Dominating the skyline for miles around, the massive airship hangars at Cardington date back to the 1930s and were home to the doomed R 101 airship. The area is a focal point for airship enthusiasts who insist that the huge Grade II listed structures are correctly called 'sheds' rather than hangars! A small airship industry is still based at Cardington today. The hangars are large enough to accommodate 8000 double decker buses with a floor area twice the size of Wembley Stadium!*

The Cowper and Newton Museum

**Orchard Side,
Market Square
Olney MK46 4AJ
☎ 01234 711516.**

Situated on the south side of the market square. Opening hours, between 1 March and 23 December are 10am to 1pm and 2pm to 5pm, Tuesdays to Saturdays, also Bank Holiday Mondays. Closed Good Friday. There is a nominal admission charge. Toilets are available on the market square.

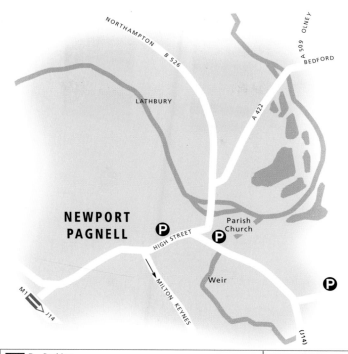

NORTHAMPTON

B 526

OLNEY

A 509

BEDFORD

LATHBURY

A 422

NEWPORT PAGNELL

Ⓟ HIGH STREET

Parish Church

Ⓟ

Weir

Ⓟ

MILTON KEYNES

M1

J14

(J14)

KEY P= Parking

SCALE = 1/2 MILE

For further information on Newport Pagnell and Olney visit the following websites:
http.www.mkheritage.co.uk/ www.mkweb.co.uk/ www.cowperandnewtonmuseum.org

Cromwell Museum

Grammar School Walk, Huntingdon
OS Grid reference TL 238718

The museum houses the best collection of material relating to Cromwell anywhere in the world and includes many items owned or directly associated with him. Guided tours are available and it is open all year except Mondays, though times vary according to season. Admission is free.
☎ 01480 375830
Wheelchair access is possible in the museum.
email: CromwellMuseum@cambridgeshire.gov.uk

Cromwell Web site:
www.olivercromwell.org

By Car: From Bedford town centre take the A428 Cambridge road to the A1 trunk road. Turn left at the roundabout and continue north on the A1 for approximately 16 kilometres (10 miles) to the A14 interchange at Brampton. Go east (right) on A14 to the first junction, B1514 (Huntingdon Race Course) for Huntingdon town centre. After passing through Brampton village, look out for Hinchingbrooke House on the left. The Cromwell family owned this house at the time Oliver was born. It is now a school with limited opening to the public. Just beyond the railway station, where the B1514 passes under the A14 concrete viaduct, the Huntingdon ring road

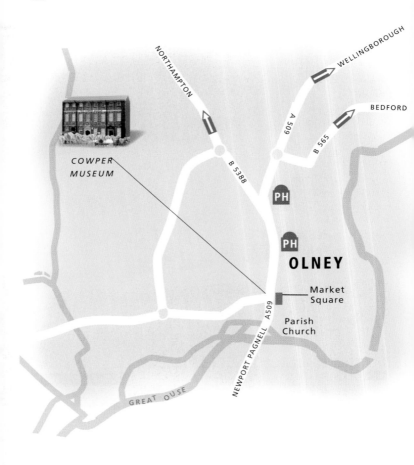

NORTHAMPTON

WELLINGBOROUGH

BEDFORD

A 509

B 565

B 5388

COWPER MUSEUM

PH

PH

OLNEY

Market Square

NEWPORT PAGNELL A509

Parish Church

GREAT OUSE

| KEY P= Parking   PH= Public House | SCALE = 1 MILE |

is reached. Follow the one way system looking out for several town centre car parks signposted, or alternatively, the riverside car park, south of the town on the banks of the Great Ouse (parking here will involve a few minutes walk into the town centre).

The Cromwell museum is in the High Street, near Market Hill, opposite All Saints Church. Huntingdon is an interesting town dating back many centuries, and there are over 150 properties of special architectural or historic interest. A town centre trail guide giving details of these sites and other useful information is available from the tourist information centre, which is in Princes Street. Public toilets are located nearby at the bus station. **Public transport** is available from Bedford Bus station to Huntingdon town centre. Travel line ☎ 0870 608 2 608

Cromwell's House

**29 St. Mary's Street
Ely Cambridgeshire
CB7 4HF**

**OS Grid reference
TL 537805**

The family home of Oliver Cromwell from 1636. This carefully restored property in the cathedral city of Ely, in the heart of the English Fens, has displays and period rooms relating to its

famous 17th century owner. It contains a Civil War exhibition as well as Cromwell's study. There is a nominal charge for admission. The house is also the local tourist information centre.
☎ 01353 662062
Website:
www.elyeastcambs.co.uk
Ely is 72 kilometres (45 miles) north east of Bedford via A428 to Cambridge then A10 for Ely. Coach and car parking is available at the Cathedral car park, which is clearly signposted.

② A cottage home in Elstow

Newly released from the parliamentary army, the wild, careless and penniless soldier moved into a home in Elstow with his young bride. The white, half-timbered cottages, with their overhanging storeys and gabled porches, are still much as Bunyan would have known them. To step into the parish church and churchyard is to step back into the seventeenth century

When Bunyan returned to the area in 1647 following his time in the army he quickly resumed his civilian life. At this time he appears to have been as careless as before, because he wrote, 'Here ... were judgments and mercy, but neither of them did awaken my soul to righteousness; wherefore I sinned still, and grew more and more rebellious against God, and careless of mine own salvation.'

According to descriptions he was quite tall with fair, reddish hair, a ruddy complexion and a quick wit. Such a lad soon found a wife and in 1649, at twenty one

Above: Picturesque cottages in the village of Elstow—referred to as Elnestou in the Domesday Book

Opposite: "The Jetty," Elstow High Street. In Bunyan's time this was a dropping off-point for the London–Bedford horse-drawn stage coach

JOHN BUNYAN
LIVED IN A COTTAGE
ON THIS SITE
1649 ~ 1655

*Top: The Abbey
church of St Mary and
St Helena, Elstow*

*Above: "Bunyan's
Cottage" before its
demolition in 1968*

years of age, he married and moved into a cottage in Elstow village.

Married life must have been a struggle, for he himself tells us: 'We came together as poor as poor might be, not having so much household stuff as a dish or spoon betwixt us both.' We do not know the name of the young bride although some think it may have been Mary, the name given to their first daughter. Whether that is so or not, she seems to have been capable of handling her husband's 'wild and wilful ways.' Her godly father had given her as a dowry two books, *The Plain Man's Pathway to Heaven*, written by Arthur Dent, a minister from Shoebury in Essex, in 1601. The writer called it a 'Little Sermon' yet it amounted to a 423 page study of a variety of religious topics, including worldly corruption, damnation of the wicked, sin and salvation! The other book, *The Practise of Piety*, was published in 1612 by Dr. Lewis Bayley, who later became Bishop of Bangor. It enjoyed a wide reputation with Puritans as well as with churchmen, and the author described it as 'A Plain Description of the Essence and Attributes of God, out of the holy Scripture'. Bunyan's wife often read from these to John; 'wherein I also found some things that were somewhat pleasing to me; but all this while I met with no conviction.'

She also managed to get John to attend church regularly: 'I fell in very eagerly with the religion of the times; to wit, to go to church twice a day, and that too with the foremost; and there should very devoutly, both say and sing as others did, yet retaining my wicked life.' However, everything connected to the church made him very superstitious, and at this period in his life his imagination worked overtime: 'But all this while, I was not sensible of the danger and evil of sin.' He tells us he was the ringleader of the local youth gangs, and he had few equals for swearing, lying and cursing. John would often be troubled by the sermons preached by the parson, Christopher Hall, yet following a good meal prepared by his loving wife, he would soon shake the thoughts out of his mind and join his friends on the village green.

One particular Sunday, Christopher Hall, who was appointed priest at Elstow church in 1639, had delivered a powerful sermon against Sunday sport—a practice hated by the Puritans. John, now a lover of Hall's sermons, was greatly troubled by this and he returned to his cottage distressed, thinking Hall had preached to particularly show him his wicked life. However,

Above: Sixteenth century cottages in Elstow High Street looking towards Bedford. Facing the pink cottage is the site of Bunyan's home 1649–1655

Above: Elstow Green and Moot Hall (early 16th century)
Opposite: Drawing of Elstow Manor built for Sir Thomas Hillersden

once again after a good meal he joined his friends on the village green to play *tip-cat*, an old English form of rounders. In his autobiography he continues, 'As I was in the midst of a game at cat, and having struck it one blow from the hole, just as I was about to strike it the second time, a voice did suddenly dart from heaven into my soul, which said, "Wilt thou leave thy sins and go to heaven, or have thy sins and go to hell?" At this I was put to an exceeding maze; wherefore, leaving my cat upon the ground, I looked up to heaven, and was as if I had, with the eyes of my understanding, seen the Lord Jesus looking down upon me.'

Bunyan entered a period of deep despair and spiritual uncertainty. It was during this time, as he was standing at a neighbour's shop-window one day, cursing and swearing, and playing the fool, that the owner of the store overheard him. She was a notable ungodly person herself, but was so shocked and frightened at the way the young Bunyan spoke that she told him he was the most ungodly fellow for swearing that she had ever heard in all her life! She said that by behaviour like this, he would affect all the youth in the whole town, if they came into his company.

Eventually, although Bunyan continued taking part in village games, his foul language and boasting was gradually cured. He began to read the Bible with his wife, especially the Old Testament, and slowly an outward reformation was noticed by those that knew him.

Elstow

The village of Elstow is just 3.5 kilometres (2 miles) from the centre of Bedford but today the county town's urban sprawl spills obtrusively into the village without any obvious interruption. In the 17th century it would certainly have been a pleasant walk through country meadows from the southern edge of the town at St. John's to the village where John Bunyan was to begin his married life.

Elstow, where lace-making was at one time a notable industry, was already well established by John Bunyan's time. The Domesday Book, written in 1086 at the command of William the Conqueror, records the village as Elnestou, or Helenstow, meaning 'Helen's Place'. The name is derived from the dedication of an early village church to Helena, mother of the Roman emperor, Constantine. By the

17th century Helenstow had, however, been abbreviated to its current form.

William the Conqueror's niece, Countess Judith, the widow of Waltheof, Earl of Huntingdon, founded the Benedictine Abbey of Elstow in about 1078-86. It was probably an expression of remorse following her betrayal of Waltheof who was beheaded for conspiracy against the King. An abbess and around thirty nuns occupied the abbey at Elstow until the mid 16th century at which time the property and estates it owned was considerable and scattered widely over several counties. One of two brasses on the floor of the south aisle in the present parish church, depicts Elizabeth Harvey, who died in 1527 and was an abbess at the abbey.

The Benedictine Abbey was finally abandoned in August 1539 just after the Dissolution of the monasteries in the reign of Henry VIII.

Plans to retain the abbey as a cathedral for Bedfordshire failed and in 1580 the majestic abbey was partially demolished as it was thought to be too large for a village church. The original chancel, high altar, chapter house, cloisters and living quarters were all dismantled. Remains of a later Renaissance style mansion, built on the site by Sir Thomas Hillersden, can be seen today immediately south of the church. It fell into disrepair in the late 18th century.

The Village Green

Elstow's half-timbered cottages in the main village street with their overhanging storeys, peaked dormers and gabled porches, are very much as they would have been in Bunyan's day. The white painted cottages opposite the village green were sympathetically renovated in the 1970s and with a new development of bungalows at

A 603

FENLAKE ⟶ SANDY

A 600 ⟶ HITCHIN

A 6 (T) AMPTHILL RD

A 5134 PROGRESS WAY

MILE ROAD

BUNYAN
(SPORTS)
CENTRE

A 421T (CAMBRIDGE) & A 1

WEST
END

CHURCH

ELSTOW

HARROWDEN

A 5134

A6 (T)

See inset map on page 34

the rear were renamed
'Bunyan's Mead'. The
archway leading through
to these bungalows,
known locally as 'The
Jetty' used to be a
coaching inn called, 'The

White Lion'. It was a
popular stopping point for
horse drawn coaches on
route between Bedford
and London and at the
time Bunyan lived in the
village it would have been
a focal point in village life.
Just two of several inns
that once stood in Elstow
survive, 'The Red Lion' and

'The Swan'. Both serve a
selection of food and
drinks, although 'The Red
Lion' boasts a family
restaurant as well. Most of
the buildings on this part
of Elstow's High Street,
particularly on the east
side, are of the 16th
century period and would
certainly have been known
to John Bunyan.

The main street has a
lane leading off to the
village green, which is
fringed with chestnut trees
and in the middle of which
is the stump of the old
market-cross. Country fairs
were a common feature on
this open land at the time
Bunyan knew it, and it is
most probable this was in
his mind when he vividly
depicted Vanity Fair in *The*

Pilgrim's Progress. As late
as the turn of the 20th
century a country fair was
still occasionally staged on
the village green. Until the
1980s, local farmers would
often put out their cattle
to graze on this piece of
common land.

At the eastern end of
the green stands the
'Moot Hall,' a quaint brick
and timber building, with
a projecting upper
storey—a good example
of 16th century
architecture, although the
exact date of its origin is
unclear. The ground floor
of the building was at one
time six individual lock-up
shops and evidence of this
can still be seen. The first
floor was at one time used
for village dancing, and

during the 19th century it was a venue for nonconformist worship, as well as a school. The building was completely restored in 1951 by Bedfordshire County Council as their contribution to the Festival of Britain year. It is now a museum of local 17th century life, and houses items with connections to John Bunyan including a pentagonal pulpit used by Christopher Hall, the parish priest, whose Puritan sermons had a great effect on Bunyan.

The Parish Church

The church of St. Mary's and St. Helena's, Elstow, which was extensively restored in 1880 at a cost of £14000 is where John Bunyan and his two eldest children were baptised as infants. It stands in a commanding position on the south side of the village green. Entrance to the church today is via the west end. To the left of this main doorway in the northwest corner of the building can be seen an old oak door believed to be the inspiration for Bunyan's Wicket Gate in *The Pilgrim's Progress*.

The nave is only a part of the original nunnery abbey, hence its loftiness and grandeur, with well proportioned arches. The octagonal font in which Bunyan was christened can still be seen at the west end of the north aisle. At the east end are two stained glass windows to the memory of Bunyan. The north window depicts scenes from Bunyan's book, *The Holy War*, whilst the other window in the south aisle shows various scenes from *The Pilgrim's Progress*. Both were designed and installed in the late nineteenth century. Below the window in the south aisle, known as the Bunyan chapel, is a communion table and altar rail in use in the church in the 17th century when the Bunyan family worshipped here regularly. Today this chapel is also dedicated to those who were prisoners in the Far East during the second world war and the wooden reredos was given by the Far East Prisoners of War Association. Unusually, this Early English and Norman church has a detached belfry, or 'steeple-house', and contains six bells. It dates back to the 13th century, although the upper section seen today, is a later 15th or 16th century construction. It is commonly believed that John Bunyan rang the fifth

Above: The stump of the Market Cross on Elstow Village Green. It was near to this site that Bunyan played tip-cat and had his visionary experience

bell and it is still known as the 'Bunyan Bell' today. The bell tower is thought to have been in Bunyan's thinking when he describes Beelzebub's castle in *The Pilgrim's Progress*.

Near to the base of the west wall of the tower there can be found a Cross of Sanctuary. Beyond this point safety was assured for those who were fleeing from the law in medieval times. Church law then became their protectorate against arrest or violence.

A similar example of a church nave with a separate bell tower can be seen at the village of Marston Moretaine, five miles to the west of Elstow.

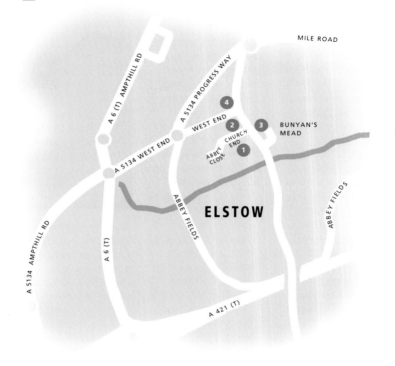

KEY ❶ ❷ ❸ ❹ **see notes below**   **SCALE = 1/4 MILE**

TRAVEL INFORMATION

Elstow

**OS Grid Reference
TL 048 475**

1 Elstow Abbey Church. On the south side of the village green. The font where John Bunyan was christened in 1628 can still be seen as well as two stained glass windows depicting scenes from *The Pilgrim's Progress* and *The Holy War.* Beyond the church are the remains of the old abbey and Hillersden Manor. The keys

to the church are available from the Vicarage or 209, Church End, (in the row of cottages beyond the church car park) at reasonable times.

2 Moot Hall. A 16th century half-timbered building on the village green. It now contains various exhibits,

illustrations and other artefacts related to 17th century Bedfordshire life and John Bunyan.

Open April–September, Tues–Thurs and Bank Holidays, 1–4pm. Nominal admission charge.
☎ 01234 266889 for more information or group bookings.

3 Bunyan's Mead Cottages. A row of Tudor cottages stand on the east side of the High Street opposite the village green. They were restored to the way they might have looked in the mid

May Day

Elstow, Bedfordshire, is widely known for its May festival and maypole dancing on the village green. In medieval and Tudor times, May Day, the first day of May, was a public holiday in England and celebrations for the coming of summer were often observed. During the time of political turmoil in the 17th century and following the Civil War, the Puritans halted May Day celebrations. However, when Charles II became king, a giant maypole was erected in the Strand, in London in May 1661 and maypoles and country dancing once again became a common feature of English country life.

In more recent times, once a year in early May, local village school children walked in procession along Elstow High Street behind a paper flowered coach, each carrying a branch covered in paper flowers for a May Festival on the village green. A 'May Queen' would be crowned, and this was followed by dancing to traditional English music around the maypole with brightly coloured ribbons. The Elstow May Festival continued well into the twentieth century; even during the Second World War the yearly excitement around the maypole went ahead. However, at the end of the 1970s the festivities on Elstow green ceased.

17th century by Bedford Borough Council in the 1970s, after being sold by the Whitbread estate for £1 on condition they were renovated.

4 Site of Bunyan's Cottage. Demolished in 1968, a plaque marks the spot where the little cottage once stood to the right of the vehicle access to the St. Helena Restaurant, High Street (north).

By Car: Elstow is 3.5 kilometres (2 miles) south of Bedford town centre via

JOHN BUNYAN
LIVED IN A COTTAGE
ON THIS SITE
1649 ~ 1655

the A6 (Luton). Follow the brown direction signs in Elstow for the Moot Hall. Ample car parking is available at the west end of the church or at the Moot Hall.

By Public transport: Bus service No 143/144 Bedford Bus Station Bay 7 to Elstow Red Lion (Not Sundays). Bedford Town Service 105/106 from town centre to Mile Road Bedford. ☎ 0870 608 2 608 for timetable and fare information.

Note: The road signs marked 'Bunyan Centre' in the vicinity of Elstow, give directions to a local sports and leisure complex of that name and bear no relation to John Bunyan heritage.

③ Out of the Slough of Despond

It was in the church of St John's in Bedford that Bunyan sat and listened to the teaching of pastor John Gifford—a man whose life had been as reckless as that of John Bunyan himself. In Gifford's home John came to a clearer understanding of his Christian faith

Following the dramatic vision experience on the village green, John Bunyan still continued bell-ringing in the Elstow church tower. He became uneasy about the whole issue of bell-ringing, however, saying that 'such practice was but vain'. He began to think, what if one of the bells should fall? So, he chose to stand under a main beam of the steeple, thinking that there he would be more secure. However, the thought then came to him that if a bell fell whilst it was swinging, it might still fall and crush him. To avoid this he pulled the rope from the steeple doorway where he felt safer. Eventually though, he thought that the steeple itself could fall, so he gave up bell-ringing altogether! It proved much harder to sacrifice dancing, however, a pastime of which he was very fond, but after a year his conscience forced him to stop this activity too.

John and his wife were obviously thrilled at the birth of their first child Mary, who was christened by Christopher Hall on the 20 July 1650. But their joy soon turned to sadness when they realised the little girl was blind.

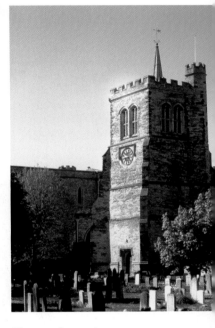

Above and opposite:
Elstow Church Belfry
stands as a completely
separate structure
alongside the main
church building. As a
bell-ringer here,
Bunyan was afraid
that the tower might
fall on him!

This was a severe blow to the couple and it added to John's burdens at that time, for he later wrote, 'My poor blind child, who lay nearer my heart than all I had beside'.

Village life

Life in general in those 17th century years was far different from today. The homes of villagers would be sparsely furnished. (A typical example of a cottage living room in Bunyan's day can be seen in the Moot Hall museum on Elstow green). The clothing worn by country people changed very little, they made clothes that were practical and meant to last and were usually plain dark colours. To modern minds their clothing would have seemed impractical and cumbersome.

People would not generally travel far beyond the boundaries of their home village. However, because of the close proximity to Bedford, the villagers of Elstow would probably have visited the town regularly.

The 17th century village would have been an important trading centre with many different occupations being practised. Men in the village would work nearby on the land or, as with Bunyan, were craftsmen who specialised in various trades.

Carpenters, locksmiths, ploughwrights, thatchers and wheelwrights were everywhere. Often the trade descended in families, as did Bunyan's craft of mending pots and pans. There was a blacksmith at Elstow in the time of Bunyan; the village smithy was at the southern end of the High Street, next to the bridge that crossed the brook, until just after the Second World War. It has since been demolished. More unusual in those days, a mat-maker is recorded to have worked in Elstow. The art of mat making involved the weaving of rushes together to form simple floor coverings. Reeds used for this craft would grow abundantly in the nearby brook. The traditional craft of lace-making was another popular cottage industry at the time in Bedfordshire. The 17th century was a buoyant period for the craft locally, and records show that even children were taught it to bolster the income for the family. Examples and more information of local lace making and other local crafts can be seen in the Bedford Museum, Castle Lane, Bedford.

Pictured above: Typical 17th century dress

Opposite page: Bunyan's Anvil bears the inscription, 'J Bunyan Helstowe, 1647'

Godly living and a new birth

Bunyan's simple occupation took him to surrounding villages and into the town of Bedford itself. Often the tinker's voice would be heard as he cried, 'Pots to mend, knives to grind—any work for a tinker?' (A brazier's anvil that Bunyan made for himself, which he would probably have carried on his back, can be seen in the Bunyan Museum, Bedford).

Inwardly, his spiritual struggles continued and increased. But Bunyan was nevertheless proud of his new-found outward godliness. He made a great determination to live a holy life in line with the Ten Commandments, and thought that even God would be pleased at that! He was yet to learn, like Martin Luther, that justification comes only by faith in the sin-atoning work of Jesus Christ, the *only* sin-bearer.

One day as he was walking through Bedford town on business, John paused, overhearing three or four women sitting at a doorway in the sunshine; they were talking about God. He thought that now as he was a 'brisk talker in matters of religion', he might join them. But as they continued their conversation his heart sank, for he realised that he did not understand their discussion. 'They were far above, out of my reach.'

The women were speaking of a *new birth* and the promises of God. They were dissatisfied with themselves and their own righteousness, and spoke of the love of the Lord Jesus as a defence against the temptations of the Devil. It seemed to John that they had found a new world. They had—it was the world of truth and salvation through Jesus Christ. This experience shook John and he began to mistrust his own self-righteousness and pride. He now thought of himself as a 'poor painted hypocrite'. It was however, to be some time before he came into full assurance of saving faith. He said of this time: 'I began to look into the Bible with new eyes, and read as I never did before; and especially the epistles of the apostle Paul were sweet and pleasant to me; and, indeed, I was then never out of the Bible, either by reading or meditation; still crying out to God, that I might know the truth, and way to heaven and glory.'

Bunyan's spiritual conflicts and struggles persisted over the coming months. More and more he wondered whether or not he was saved or whether it was 'too late'?

He eventually met with those Bedford women and soon gained real spiritual instruction and encouragement from them.

The little group of women were among the twelve founding members of John Gifford's Independent church in Bedford, and they informed their pastor of the misery and spiritual uncertainty that Bunyan was experiencing.

The Independent dissenters were then meeting in the parish church of St. John, at the southern end of the town. The 'Royalist' rector of St. John's was removed in 1653 and eventually Gifford was given use of the church and rectory. Gifford invited the twenty-five year old Elstow tinker to his rectory home in St. John's Street, and listened to his story and spiritual anxiety. Bunyan began attending the independent congregational St. John's church regularly, where he found true fellowship and friendship and slowly saw for himself, the 'preciousness of Christ' through the ministry of John Gifford. Bunyan wrote of his new spiritual guide: 'I sat under the ministry of holy Mr. Gifford, whose doctrine, by God's grace, was much for my stability. This man made it much his business to deliver the people of God from all those faults and unsound rests that, by nature, we are prone to take and make to our souls … But, oh! now, how was my soul led from truth to truth by God.'

Church Membership

Bunyan continued to struggle with doubts and a lack of assurance of Christian faith as he watched other men and women who had been converted. However, eventually, he became fully established in his faith, and the words of the apostle Paul, 'My grace is sufficient for thee,' (2 Corinthians 12: 9 AV) were often in his mind at this period. John saw that Jesus Christ was his only hope of salvation and he concluded, 'I have cause to say, "Praise ye the LORD. Praise God in his sanctuary: praise him in the firmament of his power. Praise

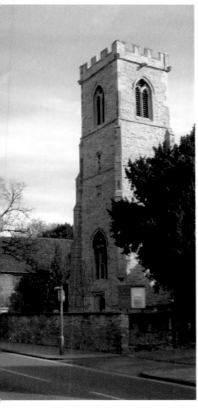

him for his mighty acts: praise him according to his excellent greatness"' (Psalm 150:1,2 AV). He showed that he had a great love for the Bible as well, for he says in *Grace Abounding:* 'The scriptures now also were wonderful things unto me; I saw that the truth and verity of them were the keys of the kingdom of heaven.'

As the weeks went by John came to the conclusion that he should become a member of the fellowship at the independent congregation at St. John's. It is generally thought that he was baptised by full immersion.

Opposite page: Bedford High Street today looking north from St. Paul's Square

Left: St. John's Church, Bedford. Bunyan attended here from 1653

Top: St. John's Rectory. 'The Interpreter's House'

Pastor John Gifford

The life and conversion of Gifford is itself an interesting account. He had been a major in the Royalist Army during the Civil War and was a notorious blasphemer, drunkard and gambler. John Gifford was one of fourteen hundred Royalist soldiers who surrendered during a battle at Maidstone in Kent. Although most of them were eventually released, because of his military rank, Gifford was a conspicuous candidate for punishment. He and eleven others were detained in Maidstone Gaol to await the gallows.

The night before his execution by Parliamentary forces, his sister visited him and found all the guards in a drunken sleep, so she helped him to escape. He hid for three days in a ditch, until the search for him was over, then, after a time in London wearing a disguise and hiding at the homes of Royalist friends, he eventually came to Bedford, married, and began a new life as a doctor.

He was still at this time a heavy drinker and gambler, and often lost his bets. This usually sent him into a temper and he would return to his home in a rage. One night, after losing an exceptionally large sum of money, he was in a drunken frenzy and began to utter desperate blasphemies against God and came very near to suicide. Then followed a remarkable conversion. For some unexplained reason he read a book by the Puritan writer, Thomas Bolton, a Fellow of Brasenose College, Oxford, which affected him deeply. He began to meet with other Puritans in the town and eventually gave up his medical practice in Bedford to become the first pastor of the nonconformist congregation in 1650.

While Gifford was pastor of the Independent church, John Bunyan found him to be a most helpful interpreter of the Bible and he gained great teaching from Gifford's ministry and conversations with him in the St. John's rectory during his conversion. John Gifford's pastorate lasted just five years. He died in September 1655 and was buried in the churchyard at St. John's, Bedford. Today, the exact location of his grave is not known.

sometime during 1653 in a little inlet of the River Ouse at Duck Mill, the baptising place customarily used by the Bedford Baptists although he never directly refers to such an incident taking place in his writings. It would probably have been conducted by John Gifford at night so as to avoid a breach of the peace—with lookouts stationed in strategic positions, all of which highlights the difficulties for the nonconformists in those troubled times.

Some still question today whether John Bunyan was really a Baptist at all! There can be no doubt that Bunyan had no time for denominational titles. He once said, 'As for those titles of Anabaptists, Independents, Presbyterians, or the like, I conclude that they come neither from Jerusalem nor from Antioch, ... for they naturally tend to division.' In fact, it would probably be safer to call Bunyan a baptist rather than a Baptist. He was baptised as a

Above and Left: *Baptism Site, Duck Mill, Bedford*

Top: *The waterway near the baptism site is a hive of activity for local canoeist groups*

believing adult and he taught that baptism should be administered only to those who had heard and believed the gospel personally. However, he did not believe that either baptism or the Lord's Supper should divide true Christians. Bunyan defended the gospel alone as the basis of Christian unity. When he involved himself in controversy, he did so because he saw a challenge to the gospel itself. Bunyan was a baptist in the sense that he held to what became the foundational tenets of Baptists. He was committed to God's word—the Bible—first and foremost; he held to a congregational form of church government, where every member played their part in decision making; and he strongly emphasized justification by faith in Christ alone. He was far more interested in God's glory and man's salvation than he was in what he saw as restrictive denominational labels or titles.

④ Just north of the river

Wherever and whenever Bunyan preached, whether outside, in cottages or in barns, the crowds would gather. Not all were impressed, however, and with tragedy in his home and the political storm clouds gathering, life was certain to change forever

On 14 April 1654 a second daughter, Elizabeth, was born to John and his wife. They were delighted that she was a healthy child without the disability or sickness that her elder sister Mary had. In spite of John's baptist convictions he followed the custom of the day and the baby was christened at the Abbey church in the village and her name duly registered.

The family still lived in the little roadside cottage at Elstow with its lean-to forge and workshop but a year after Elizabeth was born they left their home at Elstow, where they had lived for over six years, and moved to a house in the parish of St. Cuthbert's, in Bedford, just north of the river Ouse. It was a meagre dwelling with two living-rooms on either side of the front door and a single gable window above. The room to the right of the front door became known as 'Bunyan's Parlour', and over the fireplace were inscribed the initials 'JB'. The house was demolished in 1838; however, a wall plaque on the present building marks the spot where the little cottage once stood.

ON THIS SITE STOOD THE COTTAGE WHERE JOHN BUNYAN LIVED FROM 1655

Top: The St. Cuthberts Street home of Bunyan, pictured before demolition in 1838
***Above:** The same site today*

***Left:** The plaque marking the site of Bunyan's Bedford home*

***Opposite:** Waters' edge*

John Gifford's death

John Bunyan decided to move from Elstow into the town to enable him to attend John Gifford's church more easily. Gifford had been pastor at the independent church in St. John's for five years and was a great influence not only in Bedford but in surrounding villages as well. Villagers in Elstow, for example, saw the remarkable change that had come over Bunyan and as a result flocked to hear the preacher who had been his spiritual teacher over the last few years. Mr Gifford was thought to be the inspiration for the Interpreter in Bunyan's *Pilgrim's Progress*.

John Gifford died in September 1655 and was buried in the graveyard at St. John's church. It was a sad loss to the church and he was greatly mourned in Bedford and the surrounding area. John Bunyan particularly felt the loss of the converted soldier turned preacher, who had led him to true faith in Jesus Christ.

Bedford town

Since earliest times Bedford, as its very name suggests, has been an important crossing point of the river that flows through its centre today. The county town is situated just one hour north from London by rail and is midway between the university centres of Oxford and Cambridge. It currently has a population of around 110,000.

The River Great Ouse which is navigable from here to the North Sea, some ninety miles north east, meanders majestically through the heart of the town, attracting visitors to its beautiful Victorian styled embankment with tree-lined paths, flower displays and open parkland which stretches out for over half a mile east from the elegant white town road bridge. The bridge was built in the early 19th century to replace the medieval stone bridge with its lock-up on the centre that had an infamous connection with John Bunyan. The bridge has been widened since then. Also dating from the 1800s is the unique

Above left: The Embankment, Bedford

Right: The Suspension Bridge, Bedford

The young preacher

The church at Bedford called another pastor following the death of Gifford. John Burton was appointed in January 1656, although he did not enjoy good health. From May that year the church began keeping regular minutes of meetings in a church book and John Bunyan's name appears nineteenth in the list of members.

Bunyan began preaching about this time. He knew it was a God-given gift, and he entered into it with great humility. He tells us, 'After this, sometimes when some of them did go into the country to teach, they would also that I should go with them; where, though as yet I did not, nor durst not, make use of my gift in an open way, yet more privately still as I came amongst the good people in those places, I did sometimes speak a word of admonition unto them also.'

The church soon realised the

suspension footbridge, a famous Bedford landmark that spans the river at the very heart of the embankment gardens.

There are three road bridges that cross the river in Bedford, the last most recent, known as Newnham bridge, was opened in 1974 to relieve traffic from the centre of the town.

The borough received its charter from the crown in the late 12th century, during the reign of Henry II. It has been a market town for many centuries and today a market is held every Wednesday and Saturday on the banks of the river, in the vicinity of the modern shopping area. Much of the centre of the town has been rebuilt since Bunyan walked its streets; yet remarkably the street layout as shown on 17th century maps has remained largely as it was

then. Bunyan would still recognise several of the churches in Bedford. The church of St. Paul's with its majestic spire that can be seen distinctively on approach to the town, is the largest and stands in its square by the civic buildings. St. Peter's church in the north of the town, behind Bunyan's statue, is a Saxon structure, and still bears the marks of a Danish invasion at the time of the Vikings who sailed up the river plundering as they went.

Following the Norman Conquest a castle was built on the banks of the river but all that remains of this today is the castle mound in the grounds of the town museum.

Another Saxon church is sited just south of the river, St. Mary's, which is now redundant and has been converted for use as an archaeology centre. A few hundred metres further south, where in Bunyan's day would have been the edge of the town, is St. John's church, known so well to him.

spiritual assets of the young Bunyan, and during the year 1656 in St. John's church, he was specifically appointed by the assembled church members, 'after some solemn prayer to the Lord', to the office of public preaching. All through this period of his life, his love and knowledge of the scriptures continued to increase dramatically. Within a short time Bunyan began an itinerant ministry, preaching in the open air, in houses, cottages and barns and even in parish churches, probably travelling around on horseback. A number of village chapels around Bedfordshire and the neighbouring counties of Cambridge, Hertford, Buckingham and Huntingdon lay claim to their foundation through the preaching and teaching of John Bunyan. The Bible was the basis of his ministry and he constantly emphasised conviction of sin and obedience to the word of God. In *Grace Abounding* he himself says of this period: 'I went for the space of two years, crying out against men's sins, and their fearful state because of them.'.

Much to his amazement crowds flocked to hear him by the hundred, and God powerfully used his ministry though he was not without critics, for he tells us: 'When I went first to preach the word abroad, the doctors and priests of the country did open wide against me.' Some said the tinker prated rather than preached, while others queried by what authority he dared to preach. Bunyan eloquently and forthrightly argued with them saying that God alone and the Independent church at Bedford had called him to preach. He was now twenty-eight years old and during this year, 1656, the Bunyans had their third child, a son, whom they named John.

Bunyan appears to have been appointed a deacon of the church at St. John's in 1657, again underlining the qualities and gifts that John possessed as a future leader of the church, although he continued his employment as a tinker at this time.

Troubled times

A fourth child, Thomas, was born in 1658. However, all was not well. Following the birth of Thomas, his wife's already frail health began to decline rapidly, and before Bunyan was thirty years old she died. He was heartbroken.

How could he go on? How could he cope alone? How could he attend to the needs of four young children? But especially, how could he meet the needs of his beloved blind daughter Mary?

Another tragedy was to hit Bunyan, for in September 1660 John Burton died and once again the Bedford people were without a pastor. But worse still, the independent congregation suddenly lost the use of the building itself. With little warning a Church of England rector was installed at St. John's and the pastor-less independents not only had to find a new pastor but also a new meeting place. The congregation now met for worship wherever they could, in a barn, a borrowed stable or in a cowshed.

For John Bunyan, these were very dark days indeed, especially as he could see a far more ominous storm rapidly gathering. He became increasingly concerned for the welfare and upbringing of his family and determined, for their sake, as well as for his own, that he must remarry. He did, in 1660 just as the storm was about to break.

National change

Britain was entering a crucial period nationally. Oliver Cromwell, who had led the popular revolt against the monarchy, was dying. His son took his place, but when Oliver died in 1658, Richard soon showed he did not possess the leadership qualities of his father, and he eventually lost support and resigned.

Opposite page:
A drawing of Bunyan preaching in Bedford, October, 1659. Note the Swan Inn—now the Swan Hotel—on the far left and the town lock-up on the river bridge in the distance

Right: *St. Paul's Square today showing the statue of John Howard*

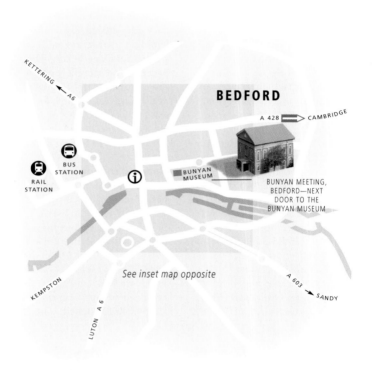

KETTERING ← A 6

BEDFORD

A 428 → CAMBRIDGE

BUS
STATION

RAIL
STATION

ⓘ

BUNYAN
MUSEUM

BUNYAN MEETING,
BEDFORD—NEXT
DOOR TO THE
BUNYAN MUSEUM

See inset map opposite

KEMPSTON

LUTON A 6

A 603 → SANDY

SCALE = 1 MILE

The restoration of the monarchy was now inevitable. England had been a commonwealth since 1649 following the public execution of Charles I at Whitehall on a snowy morning in January that year. By the spring of 1660, the majority of the country's leaders realised that his second son, also named Charles, should be invited to become Charles II of England. Charles, a dark-haired, swarthy character entered Britain following eight years of exile in Europe on 25 May 1660. He told the people as he came ashore at Dover that the Bible was the thing he loved most—not the greatest truth to come from the lips of this particular monarch! Great crowds gathered as he made his way up to London where he arrived on 29 May 1660, his thirtieth birthday.

England was overjoyed at having a King again. However, royal powers and privileges had been severely limited during the Commonwealth. The Long Parliament that had sat through the uncertain years of the Civil War was dissolved and the establishment then sought to be rid of the Puritans once and for all!

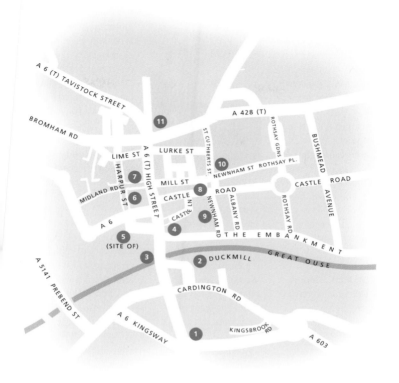

KEY ① ② ③ etc. see notes on pages 52-54

SCALE = 1/2 MILE

TRAVEL INFORMATION

Bedford Town Centre

**OS Grid Reference
TL 050 485**

General Information

Bedford is situated 80 kilometres (50 miles) north of London mid-way between the university cities of Cambridge and Oxford. There are excellent road and rail connections to the area with the main routes from London to the north passing through the county.

The M1 motorway, Junction 13, is 14.5 kilometres (9 miles) west of the town centre whilst the A1 trunk road is 13 kilometres (8 miles) to the east.

Thameslink trains from Brighton, Gatwick airport and the centre of London terminate at Bedford. (www.thameslink.co.uk) Midland Mainline rail services from St. Pancras station, London, Leicester and Sheffield pass through

Bedford. The Marston Vale rail line (Milton Keynes via Bletchley) also runs into Bedford Midland station. National Rail enquiries ☎ 0345 48 49 50 www.railtrack.co.uk London-Luton Airport (Rail station—Luton Airport Parkway) is 32 kilometres (20 miles) south of Bedford. Airport information desk ☎ 01582 405100 www.london-luton.com

A coach park is situated in Castle Lane behind Bunyan Meeting Free

Church. Town centre car parking is also available in Castle Lane and in a multi-storey car park in Lurke Street, behind the properties opposite the main entrance to the church. Public toilets are located in St. Paul's Square, opposite the Corn Exchange, and the east end of Silver Street near the site of the old Town Gaol. Toilet facilities are also available in the Bunyan museum.

side of St. John's Street, Bedford, half a kilometre south of the river.

See Pages 82-83

2 Baptism Site. It is
widely believed that John Bunyan was baptised in this backwater of the Great Ouse, just south of the weir bridge at Duck Mill. A plaque is positioned on the stone wall above the waterline describing the spot. John Bunyan does not refer to

his baptism directly in any of his writings or his autobiography. The site can be found at the end of Chethams, a close that runs off of Cardington Road, behind Dame Alice School.

3 Town Bridge. The
present elegant town bridge was opened to traffic in 1835 and widened in the late 1930s. It replaced a stone bridge, which was first built in the 13th century but had been rebuilt on several occasions. A building on the centre of the old bridge is thought to be where Bunyan was held during the 1680s and wrote his famous book, *The Pilgrim's Progress,* though today this is questionable. On the north side of the east

1 St. John's Church.
and the Interpreter's House.

St. John's Church and Rectory. The home of John Gifford, whose ministry was most helpful to Bunyan at the time of his conversion, stands prominently on the east

parapet of the bridge is a plaque relating to John Bunyan and his writings.

4 Swan Hotel.
The main staircase in the hotel is said to have come

from Houghton House, Ampthill, which was Bunyan's 'House Beautiful'. It was in a former building on this same site that Elizabeth Bunyan pleaded for her husband's pardon during his incarceration in Bedford Gaol.

5 Chapel of Herne.
Nothing remains of the medieval building where John Bunyan faced the Bedford magistrates during the Quarter Session. The building stood where the modern Town Hall office block now stands at the south-west corner of St. Paul's Square. (The statue on the old market square in front of St. Paul's church, near to the Piazza, is to the memory of John Howard, the 18th century

philanthropist and prison reformer who lived in the nearby village of Cardington. His town house stands next to the Bunyan museum in Mill Street, Bedford).

6 Bedford Central Library.
In the entrance hall of the library is a modern wall mural which depicts scenes from *The Pilgrim's Progress*. The library has an extensive collection of books relating to John Bunyan, including early editions of *The Pilgrim's Progress*. Opposite the library is an imposing early Victorian facade designed by the architect, Edward Blore. It is all that remains of Bedford Modern School, which stood on the site for over a hundred and forty years until it was replaced by a purpose built centre on the north fringes of the town in 1974. The Harpur Street area was cleared for a new shopping complex and the impressive frontage was retained.

7 County Gaol.
A plaque in the pavement on the corner of High Street and Silver Street marks the spot where the county gaol stood in the 17th century. It was demolished in 1801. John Bunyan was imprisoned here between 1660 and 1672 and from 1676 to 1677. Conditions were dreadful, dirty and overcrowded, though Bunyan never complained of that. Some privileges were given to the prisoners, which in Bunyan's case included family visits with supplementary food and drink, brought in by his blind daughter, Mary.

8 Bunyan Meeting Church and Museum.
Bunyan Meeting Free Church in Mill Street was opened in 1850 replacing a meeting house that had stood on the site since 1707. On this spot in 1672 stood a barn in an orchard, which was all purchased by a member of

Bunyan Museum

Bunyan's congregation for the sum of £90. The barn was converted to be the first meeting place of Bunyan's independent congregation following his release from gaol that year.

In the church itself can be seen part of the communion table used in Bunyan's day, and stained glass windows depicting scenes from Bunyan's works. The church is open to visitors between 10.00am and 4.00pm Tuesdays to Saturdays.

The adjoining Bunyan Museum was opened in 1998 and allows visitors to walk through different areas alluding to Bunyan's life and times. Artefacts associated with the famous 17th century preacher and pastor can be seen, as well as a collection of *The Pilgrim's Progress* in many different languages. Although the museum is sited on the first floor, there is a chair-lift available.

The museum is open from 11.00 am to 4.00 pm Tuesdays to Saturdays from March to the end of October.

For further information relating to the Bunyan Meeting Church and the museum, contact the Church Office, Bunyan Meeting Free Church, Mill Street, Bedford MK40 3EU ☎ and Fax: 01234 213722.

9 **Bedford Museum.**
The town museum in Castle Lane houses displays relating to the history and natural history of Bedford and the surrounding area. Opening hours are 11am to 5pm Tuesdays to Saturdays, and from 2pm on Bank Holidays. There is a nominal admission charge. ☎ 01234 353323

10 **Site of Bunyan's Home.**
The site of Bunyan's Bedford home is No.17 St. Cuthbert's Street, and a plaque on the wall of the present property marks the spot. John and his family moved here from Elstow in 1655. When the cottage was demolished in 1838, John's Deed of Gift, drawn up in 1685, was discovered hidden in the brickwork of the chimney. He had left his entire

estate, which amounted to very little, to his wife Elizabeth. The document is now in the Bunyan Museum, Mill Street, Bedford.

11 **Bunyan's Statue.**
At the north end of the High Street, on St. Peter's Green stands the bronze statue, which was presented to the town by the Duke of Bedford in 1874. Sir John E. Boehm sculptured the figure, which weighs over three tons and stands nine feet high. Around the pedestal are three bronze panels illustrating different scenes from *The Pilgrim's Progress.*

The Bronze doors

The doors of the Bunyan Meeting Church are copper on bronze, and were given to the Church in 1876 by Hastings, 9th Duke of Bedford. They are modelled on the Baptistry Doors at Florence, and are the work of sculptor Frederick Thrupp. The doors have ten panels, each one depicting a scene from *The Pilgrim's Progress.*

Left: Panels 5 and 6

9	10
7	8
5	6
3	4
1	2

Key to the panels

1. Christian about to leave his family.

2. Christian being welcomed at the Wicket Gate by Goodwill.

3. Christian meets the Shining Ones at the Cross.

4. Christian asleep in the arbour on Hill Difficulty.

5. Christian passing the lions on his way to the House Beautiful.

6. Christian talking with Simple, Sloth and Presumption.

7. Christian receiving his armour at the House Beautiful. (Notice the ancient weapons in the background)

8. Christian being beckoned by Demas to view his Silver Mine.

9. A composite picture of Faithful's death, and of the chariot taking him to the Celestial City.

10. Christian with Hopeful crossing the River of Death.

Notice that two panels are in the wrong order. Panel 6 should be number 4, and panel 8 should be number 9. Did the artist arrange them in this order to give a better balance, or did he make a mistake?

⑤ Into Bedford prison

The old county prison in Bedford—without heat, light or sanitation—was an awful place, and it testified to Bunyan's determination and longsuffering. Despite the injustice of his trial and the courageous actions of his young wife, John Bunyan remained a prisoner for the sake of the gospel and his conscience

Charles II solemnly declared that he would grant 'liberty to tender consciences', and many non-conformists, including John Bunyan, had no reason to doubt that these encouraging words would give opportunities for those who worshipped according to their conscience. Another encouragement at that time for John and his new wife, Elizabeth, was the prospect of their first child before Christmas, 1660. They were soon to be disappointed over both matters.

The Bedford magistrates rapidly used their powers under the new monarchy to enforce adherence to the Church of England Prayer Book. This situation put fresh pressures on the struggling Independent church at Bedford and Puritans generally throughout the country who refused to conform to the Book of Common Prayer which they considered to be too 'High Church' or even Roman Catholic.

In November 1660, John was invited to preach on a farm at Lower Samsell, a hamlet near Harlington, twelve miles south of

Above: Bunyan's Oak at Lower Samsell before the storm of 1987. Bunyan would use this as his pulpit when preaching. He was arrested half a mile northeast of here in November 1660

Left: Mute Swan

Above: The Warrant for Bunyan's arrest

Top: Harlington Manor House where Bunyan was interrogated

Bedford. He knew the district well and had often preached in the area. Not wishing to disappoint his friends there, he went, knowing that he faced possible arrest. As he arrived he was informed that the local landlord and Justice of the Peace, Francis Wingate, had already issued a warrant for his arrest. In a manuscript entitled *A Relation of the Imprisonment of Mr John Bunyan*, published in 1765 nearly eighty years after his death, Bunyan clearly describes the events that subsequently took place.

His host at Samsell was nervous and suggested that they cancel the meeting. 'No, by no means, I will not stir, neither will I have the meeting dismissed for this' declared Bunyan, 'Come, be of good cheer; let us not be daunted; our cause is good, we need not be ashamed of it; to preach God's word … even if we suffer for it.'

The meeting had hardly

commenced with prayer, when a village constable and a magistrate's assistant burst into the house and ordered the meeting to stop. A *Warrant for the Arrest of John Bunyan* was rudely thrust into his hands. Calmly, John spoke some words of encouragement and counsel to the alarmed worshippers before he was led away. As Wingate was not at home that day, John spent the night with a local friend who had offered to become surety that Bunyan would appear before the Justice at Harlington Manor the following morning.

Harlington Manor, Francis Wingate's home, stands on a crossroads in the centre of the village and dates back to 1396. On one occasion Charles II spent a night there while on one of his countrywide journeys. A brick wall surrounded the manor house with large wooden gates at the entrance.

'So on the next morning we went to the constable, and so to

Top: Cottages in Harlington

Above: The Church at Harlington

Top: A 17th century cottage in Harlington

Left: Although the old Bedford Gaol has long been demolished, its site is marked today by a well-worn pavement plaque to the front of the three storey building seen here on the high street

Bottom left: Taken from a drawing of The Chapel of Herne where Bunyan appeared before the magistrate, Sir John Kelynge

Opposite page: St Paul's Church

the justice.' Bunyan tells us he was taken into an oak panelled room in the manor house where Wingate was already waiting. 'He asked the constable what we did, where we was met together, and what we had with us? … But when the constable told him that there were only met a few of us together to preach and hear the word, and no sign of anything else, he could not well tell what to say.'

Bunyan calmly answered all the questions that were put to him that day but his defence was futile. Though certain friends tried to change Wingate's mind, 'I held my peace, and, blessed be the Lord, went away to prison, with God's comfort in my poor soul.' Under escort, John was taken twelve miles north, to the county gaol in Bedford's High Street, to await a hearing before the Justice.

Tradition has developed over the years that Bunyan was imprisoned in the town lock-up in the centre of the stone bridge that then straddled the River Ouse. There are, however, serious doubts today about this theory. The town jail was small and only suitable for petty criminals, vagrants and drunks. There were many arrested at that time for offences similar to Bunyan's. The gaol on the bridge simply could not have housed such numbers. Also, as Bunyan was not arrested in the town, but elsewhere in the county, he would most probably have been held in the county prison.

The prison, which stood on the corner of the High Street and the present Silver Street, was demolished in 1801, and no known pictures or prints of it have survived. It is believed that it had two storeys, and two cells below ground level, one of which had no natural light. It must have been bitterly cold in winter as there were no fireplaces and the prisoners would have slept on straw. Food would have been meagre and the sanitation unimaginable today. One of the imposing oak doors can now be seen in the Bunyan museum in Bedford.

News of Bunyan's arrest soon reached those who were close to him. The church members sought the help of a magistrate in Elstow, Mr Crompton. He was at first sympathetic, but eventually declined further involvement because he suspected a political offence. For Bunyan's family,

living only five minutes from the gaol, there was great sorrow. Poor Elizabeth, who was heavily pregnant with her first child, went into premature labour, and a week later gave birth to a stillborn child.

Several weeks went by before John appeared before the County Quarter Sessions in January 1661. These were held in a Gothic ecclesiastical style building, known as the Chapel of Herne, which stood on the north bank of the river at the south-west corner of St. Paul's churchyard.

On the Bench were five Royalist-sympathising local landowners, headed by Sir John Kelynge of Southill, a practising barrister. One other, Henry Chester, was the uncle of Francis Wingate. In all, it was a formidable aristocratic judiciary that Bunyan faced.

The indictment was read out to the prisoner: 'John Bunyan, of the town of Bedford, labourer ... hath devilishly and perniciously abstained from coming to church to hear Divine service, and is a common upholder of several unlawful meetings and conventicles, to the great hindrance and distraction of the good subjects of this kingdom contrary to the laws of our sovereign lord, the King.' Bunyan was then asked to reply. In his book, *A Relation of the Imprisonment of Mr John Bunyan,* he clearly details the responses and defence that he made—with conviction and good reasoning from the Bible and mostly to the confusion of the Bench.

Pictured above: The Great Ouse from Prebend Street. The Chapel of Herne stood on the site now occupied by the office block

Opposite page: It is believed that blind Mary carried soup to her imprisoned father in this salt-glazed stoneware jug

Eventually however, after consultation with the other men on the Bench, Kelynge pronounced to Bunyan, 'You must be had back again to prison, and lie there for three months following … if you do not submit to go to church to hear divine service, *and leave your preaching* you must be banished from the realm.' He concluded, angrily, 'If after such a day … you shall be found in this realm or be found to come over again without special licence from the King, you must stretch from the neck for it!—Take him away'. As Bunyan was dragged away he turned to the bench and respectfully said in a dignified voice, 'Sir, as to this matter, I am at a point with you; for if I am out of prison today, *I will preach the gospel again tomorrow—by the help of God.*'

Bunyan continues, 'Thus I departed from them, and I can truly say, I bless the Lord Jesus Christ for it that my heart was sweetly refreshed in the time of the examination…and at my returning to the prison.' He never forgot the events of that day, and sixteen years later he wrote of the courthouse, the proceedings, the judges and lawyers and gave Sir John Kelynge the inglorious title of Lord Hategood of Vanity Fair, in his famous work, *The Pilgrim's Progress.*

Bunyan in prison

John Bunyan returned to the prison and to the company of villains and vagabonds, drunks and debtors. His crime was simply breaking repressive laws that violated his conscience and belief, as he continually refused to attend the parish church and dared to preach without a licence from the bishop. John was resigned to his incarceration and probably spoke to those around him about God and preached the gospel to all who would hear him.

Life in the High Street cell was hard, but it appears that John was given some favours from the gaoler. He was allowed to see his family and he asked them to bring him his Bible and concordance and during his time in prison they supplemented his food and drink. Even his blind daughter, Mary, now eleven, managed to find her own way to the prison. An earthen jug, believed to be the one used to carry broth from the family home to the gaol, can be seen today in the Bunyan museum.

At first there were opportunities for John to leave the gaol for a few hours at a time. The church minute book of the time records that he attended some church meetings although the Bedford Independent church was now being harassed and met secretly, often in far off places such as Haynes and Gamlingay.

Above: *The Swan Hotel today*

John even managed to preach on occasions in woods, fields and isolated farm buildings! This action was very risky as rewards were offered to those who informed the authorities of the whereabouts of secret religious meetings.

In order to provide support to his family, John would spend many hours in his cell making leather laces for boots and shoes, which were sold to local traders that passed by the prison. Members of the Bedford meeting also made great efforts and sacrifice to support the Bunyan family financially and with other practical gifts.

Bunyan's own account of his imprisonment tells us that on 3 April 1661 he received a visit from the local Clerk to the Justice, Mr Paul Cobb, who had been sent in order to gain a submission before the spring Quarter-Sessions; he urged Bunyan to obey the law or else matters could only get worse!

However, after a lengthy discussion Bunyan explained that he could not agree to conform as it was against his conscience and he was happy to bear the consequences of his actions. He then thanked Mr Cobb 'for his civil and meek discoursing with me; and so we parted.'

The King's Coronation

King Charles II was crowned on 23 April 1661, which meant a postponement of the Quarter-Sessions in Bedford. It was customary for some prisoners to be released to mark the occasion, but Bunyan's name was not included. As he had not confessed either way, Kelynge had entered his silence as a confession of guilt and his appearance before the judges was delayed even further. He was now classed as a convicted criminal and the only hope of pardon now was an appeal for clemency during the twelve months that followed the coronation, although it is likely that there was an official conspiracy to keep Bunyan in prison and no plea would ever be accepted.

Elizabeth Bunyan was a great support to her husband and it is obvious that God had brought her into John's life at a crucial time. The weight of anxiety and responsibility that was placed upon her to look after four step-children was considerable and although she suffered herself with the loss of her first child she was prepared to act on the behalf of her husband with remarkable courage and persistence.

A carefully worded petition was written by John Bunyan and his wife, possibly with help of more educated members of the church. Several copies of it were made and Elizabeth undertook their distribution.

During the late spring of 1661 the courageous Elizabeth travelled to London, to the House of Lords, to present a petition to Lord Barkwood, a peer who it was thought may be able to help gain a pardon for Bunyan. After consulting with other Lords however, he told Elizabeth that her husband could only be freed at the local Assize hearings.

The Summer Assize

The Midsummer Assize was held in August 1661, at the Chapel of Herne, four months after the coronation. The two Judges were

Above: The room in Harlington Manor House where Bunyan was questioned by Francis Wingate after his arrest at Lower Samsell

Right:
Victorian
engraving
depicting John
Bunyan's wife
pleading with the
magistrates for his
release in prison
in 1662

Right:
Victorian
engraving
depicting John
Bunyan's wife
pleading with the
magistrates for his
release in prison
in 1662

Opposite page:
The minute book
of the Bunyan
Meeting Church
when Bunyan
was pastor

Sir Thomas Twisden and Sir Matthew Hale. Twisden was a hard man and conventional Royalist. It was unlikely that he would be helpful to the case. Judge Hale however, might have been expected to be more fair-minded. Six years earlier he had sat in Cromwell's Parliament and eventually was to become the Lord Chief Justice in 1671. It was known that Hale had sympathy for the dissenters amongst whom he had spent his school days.

Elizabeth Bunyan, though relatively young, was devoted to her husband and the faith and presented her case to Sir Matthew Hale. Bunyan tells us that Hale 'very mildly' received her petition and said he would do what he could but feared he could do no more. The following day as Sir Twisden's coach drove though the streets of Bedford, Elizabeth courageously threw a copy of the petition through the open window on to his lap, perhaps an unwise gesture as it made him angry! Stopping the coach he bawled at her, saying Bunyan could not be released from gaol until he relinquished preaching. Elizabeth was undeterred however and attended the Assize court whilst it was in session and during an interval she presented another copy of the petition to Judge Hale who on this occasion seemed to take more interest in the case—until a local magistrate intervened and dissuaded him.

Swan Song
Elizabeth's final endeavour on behalf of her imprisoned husband immediately followed the Midsummer Assize Session. The Swan Inn, now the Swan Hotel, was where the local gentry and landowners met with the Judges before they left the town to consider county matters. Courageously pushing her way

through officials, she climbed the stairs and entered the Swan Chamber. Above the noise in the room, in a loud voice but dignified manner, she addressed the two Judges, Sir Thomas Twisden and Judge Matthew Hale. Elizabeth explained that her husband had been falsely accused and he was not out to make trouble. For a while she successfully held up the official agenda, landowner concerns and other parish matters, pleading the case for John's release from prison. Hale was again sympathetic, but on several occasions, in reply to Elizabeth's petition, the local magistrate, Sir Henry Chester of Lidlington, reminded the Judges that Bunyan was lawfully convicted and that it was lawfully recorded.

Finally, the patience of the two Judges broke and Mrs Bunyan was asked point blank if her husband was prepared to give up preaching? Desperately she replied, 'My Lord, he dares not leave preaching as long as he can speak.' She explained that she had four young dependent stepchildren, one of which was blind, and had lost her own child in recent months. This gained a measure of respect from Judge Hale, but abruptly, Twisden interrupted saying that she was using her circumstances to gain sympathy.

The Judges summed up the matter advising they could do no more and she should apply to the King for a pardon or seek for a retrial. At this hardhearted reaction of the Judges, Elizabeth broke down. She left the room in a flood of tears to return to her poor husband in the county prison. It was the end of her concerted and brave campaign.

Before the Bedford Assizes of 1662 took place, John endeavoured to have his name entered in the calendar of offenders, so his case would come before the Judges. However, the Clerk of the Peace altered the entry, making it possible for Bunyan to remain in prison for the next four years.

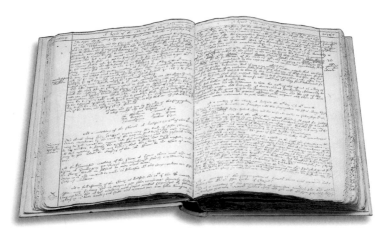

AMPTHILL

SAMSELL

UPPER SAMSELL FARM

BEDFORD

PH

BUNYAN ARRESTED ON A FARM (NOW GONE) IN THE SAMPSELL AREA

BARTON

A 6

MANOR HOUSE

BUNYAN'S OAK

SHARPENHOE

HITCHIN B

RAIL STATION

CHURCH

A 5120

B 655

JUNCTION 12

HARLINGTON

SHARPENHOE CLAPPERS

NORTH

M 1

A 6

SOUTH

SUNDON HILLS COUNTRY PARK

STREATLEY

LUTON

KEY P= Parking   **PH**= Public House   **SCALE = 2 MILES**

TRAVEL INFORMATION

For travel details regarding the County Gaol and Chapel of Herne, in Bedford, see the travel notes on page 53

Harlington village

Grid reference TL 048307

By car from Bedford:
Take the A6 towards Luton. After 17.5 kilometres (11 miles) leave the A6 at the roundabout north of Barton-le-Clay and enter

the village on the B655. After 1/2 mile at a roundabout in the centre of the village, turn right on an unclassified road for Sharpenhoe and Harlington. After 5 kilometres (3 miles) as you enter the village of Harlington, there are good views of the 'Delectable Mountains' to the left (See the details for Sharpenhoe Clappers and Sundon Country park, later in this section). At the crossroads in the centre of Harlington beyond the church, turn left for Upper Sundon. Immediately on the left is a

car park adjacent to the village hall opposite the Carpenters Arms public house.

Harlington village is just 2.5 Kilometres (1 1/2 miles) from Junction 12 of the M1 motorway. Follow the A5120 towards Flitwick and Ampthill for 1 kilometre (1/2 mile) then follow the signs for Harlington Station. At the crossroads just beyond the railway station, turn right for the village hall car park, which is immediately on the left.

Picture: Bunyan's Oak near Lower Samsell today. Bunyan was arrested
in this area in 1660

Public Transport from Bedford: Regular Thameslink trains from Bedford to Harlington station (Toddington Road). The Manor House where Bunyan was interrogated following his arrest can be seen on the corner of Toddington Road and Westoning Road (over the high brick wall). It is now a private dwelling.

The parish church of St. Mary's contains a small but fine 'Pilgrim' stained glass window and an altar table which is supported with legs made from 'Bunyan's Oak' tree (see below) and another table made from the same source.

A 3 kilometres (1–2 miles) walk to Samsell near to where Bunyan was arrested: Leave the Harlington village hall car park and head for the village church in Barton Road. At the church take the footpath to the right of the church gate across the park to rejoin Barton Road. Continue for 1 kilometre (1/2 mile) along Barton Road (houses on your left) with good open views to the right across to the Chiltern Hills —'The Delectable Mountains'. After crossing the junction with Goswell End Road, take the footpath that goes off Barton Road to the left, (behind the white cottage) into open farmland. After approximately 1 kilometre (1/2mile), you come to the site where Bunyan would preach in the open air, near to an old oak tree (now just a dead stump). A commemorative sapling has been planted nearby. It was at a farmhouse 1 kilometre (1/2 mile) beyond this spot that John Bunyan was arrested in November 1660.

6   The pen in the prison

Offered the choice of ending his preaching or remaining in prison, Bunyan chose to stay where he was, and so began his most valuable ministry of writing. *The Pilgrim's Progress* was created in the cold gloom of a town lock-up, the buildings and sites in it inspired by places in Bedfordshire that Bunyan knew and loved

John never wasted time! As well as making bootlaces to bring in a little money for his family and speaking to fellow prisoners and parishioners regarding the Christian faith, he would sit in his cell and write. For a number of years before his imprisonment, he had been responsible for several short tracts, but between 1660 to 1666 he issued nine different publications including, in 1664, *One Thing is Needful,* which was published on a single sheet and distributed by his wife and family in order to help them financially. In all, over sixty works ranging from one-page essays to masterful volumes, along with verses and rhyme were to come from Bunyan's pen during his life.

Bunyan had published his first article back in 1656, soon after his conversion. This was in response to a visit to Bedfordshire during 1654 of William Dewsbury, a national leader of the Quakers. Dewsbury had aroused interest in the religious group but Bunyan and other Puritans at that time considered their beliefs unscriptural. Bunyan condemned the group as heretical and entitled

his article *Some Gospel truths opened, according to the Scriptures, of the Divine and Human Nature of Jesus Christ … Published for the good of God's chosen ones, by that unworthy servant of Christ, John Bunyan of Bedford, by the grace of God, preacher of the Gospel of His Dear Son.* This extraordinarily long and ungainly title was a practice that the Puritans used in order to present their readers with a broad outline of the contents in the book. It was 216 pages long and showed what an outstanding knowledge of the Bible Bunyan already possessed. The publisher, Matthias Cowley, was a bookseller in Newport Pagnell, an acquaintance from the time that

Opposite: John Bunyan in Prison. A stained glass window in Bunyan Meeting Free church, Bedford. Commemorating the tercentenary of the publication of 'The Pilgrim's Progress' in February 1978

Bunyan was garrisoned in the town as a soldier.

There then followed 'tit for tat' publications between John and the Quakers including one entitled, *A Vindication of Gospel Truths Opened*, where Bunyan's obvious gift for writing was becoming apparent.

In 1658 and 1659 he published two further books. *A Few Sighs*

from Hell or the Groans of a Damned Soul was the alarming title he gave to a book written following a sermon he preached on the parable of the Rich Man and the Beggar, in Luke 16: 19-31, and contained a preface written by his friend, John Gibbs of Newport Pagnell. The second, *The Doctrine of Law and Grace Unfolded*, was a profound theological testimony, which proved to be the last book he wrote before his arrest.

A book entitled *A Discourse Touching Prayer* was published from prison in 1662. It was the basis of a sermon he preached in the gaol in which he defends spontaneous praying made with the assistance of the Holy Spirit rather than formalistic written prayers of man's invention—a clear attack on the Prayer Book.

Much of Bunyan's rhyme was rather quaint but an excerpt from a poem called *Prison Meditations*, written whilst in Bedford gaol; show the inner feelings of the imprisoned writer.

For though men keep my outward man within their locks and bars, Yet by the faith of Christ I can mount higher than the stars. Their fetters cannot spirits tame, nor tie up God from me; My faith and hope they cannot lame, above them I shall be.

Above: *The prison door from the County Gaol, demolished in 1802*

Opposite: *A scene from 'The Pilgrim's Progress,' from Cassel's Illustrated Bunyan which dates from the late Victorian era*

Grace Abounding

In 1666, Bunyan wrote of his own spiritual experience in *Grace Abounding to the Chief of Sinners*. It was a 'faithful account' of his life up to that point of time and he gave the book a very carefully worded title.

The preface opens in language similar to that of the apostle Paul's writings when *he* was in prison, in Rome: 'Children, grace be with you, Amen. I being taken from you in presence, and so tied up, that I cannot perform that duty that from God doth lie upon me ... for your further edifying and building up in faith and holiness, etc, ... greatly longing to see your safe arrival into the desired haven.' Then, Bunyan continues a sentence or two later: 'In this discourse of mine you may see much ... of the grace of God towards me. I thank God I can count it much, for it was above my sins and Satan's temptations too. I can remember my fears, and doubts, and sad months with comfort ...they bring afresh into my mind the remembrance of my great help, my great support from heaven, and the great grace that God extended to such a wretch as I.'

It took John some time to write this book but when eventually it was completed and he was satisfied with it, he showed it to his close friends who greatly approved of it. George Larkin, of Bishopsgate, London, published it the same year 1666—the year of the Great Fire of London.

First editions of the book are

extremely rare, probably as a result of the fire. Only one copy is held by the British Library, which it obtained over 200 years after the first publication. However the book went on to be one of the greatest of all spiritual autobiographies. Ernest Bacon in his book *Pilgrim and Dreamer* concluded that it made John Bunyan famous during his lifetime and brought inspiration and comfort to countless thousands in those dark days.

Literary Fame

By the time Bunyan was forty years of age in 1668 he was renowned as a writer and his works were well sought after. His preaching through the prison pen was far more widespread and effective than if he had been a free man! However, his writing was to mature with time and it was to be the latter part of his life, which saw the publication of his best-known work. The first part of *The Pilgrim's Progress* was written between the years 1672-77, followed by *The Life and Death of Mr Badman*—his third major work, which appeared in 1680, two years after *The Pilgrim's Progress* was first published.

There then followed another major work, *The Holy War*, which vividly characterises the spiritual conquests of the Christian and was published in 1682. In it we are introduced to such names as Mansoul, Captain Anything, Mr God's Peace and Diabolus—the Devil—and, of course, Emmanuel.

In Elstow Church, a stained glass memorial window at the east

STEVE DEVANE

Above: *The Holy War: section of a a stained glass window at Elstow Parish Church*

end of the nave depicts scenes from *The Holy War*. Underneath it is written,

To the memory of Bunyan and to remind all Christian people of the Holy War they should be engaged in on the side of Emmanuel.

This seems a fitting memorial to a great literary work and a great author.

In his final year on earth, Bunyan wrote no fewer than five books including, *The Jerusalem Sinner Saved* and *The Acceptable Sacrifice*, the manuscript of which was in his pocket on his last journey to London and was published after his death in 1689.

The Pilgrim's Progress

'As I walked through the wilderness of this world, I lighted on a certain place where was a den, and I laid me down in that place to sleep: and, as I slept, I dreamed a dream. I dreamed, and behold, I saw a man clothed with rags, standing in a certain place, with his face from his own house, a book in his hand, and a great burden upon his back. I looked, and saw him open the book, and read therein; and, as he read, he wept, and trembled; and, not being able longer to contain, he brake out with a lamentable cry,

saying, What shall I do?'

So begins the book that is probably the greatest allegory ever written and was to make the name of John Bunyan famous throughout the world. It was Bunyan's most notable work and is even more remarkable when we consider again the simple education and upbringing of this country tinker who lived the first twenty years of his life in an ungodly, unscholarly manner, never displaying the literary qualities of his later life.

The Pilgrim's Progress demonstrates how Bunyan had 'progressed' literally in his own life through severe temptations and spiritual doubts to salvation through Jesus Christ. He displays his great knowledge and love of the Scriptures, which were his delight to study, particularly during the days of imprisonment. Coupled with this we are shown the qualities of a wonderful mind, which encapsulated vividly, scenes, places and people that had greatly affected him during his life. Bunyan's style and careful perception of human nature holds the reader's attention throughout the book.

It is unclear when Bunyan actually began writing *The Pilgrim's Progress*. At the time of his release from prison in 1672 the work was unfinished due the heavy workload he had during four years of freedom. His preaching and exercising pastoral duties at the Bedford church had kept him very busy. It was probably not until he returned to prison in 1676 for yet another period of incarceration, that he

Right: Houghton House, near Ampthill, Bunyan's 'House Beautiful'

was able to continue writing the allegory. This second period of imprisonment ended in the summer of 1677, eight months before *The Pilgrim's Progress* was first published in February 1678. The opening phrase of the book may offer a clue to where Bunyan was imprisoned on this occasion. The 'den' is thought by some to refer to the small lock-up cell situated on the 13th century stone bridge that then crossed the river Ouse at Bedford. A brass plaque referring to this can be seen on the wall of the northern end of the east parapet on the present town bridge, opposite the Swan Hotel.

The Pilgrim's Progress is the story of a pilgrimage through this world to the world to come, and tells of the varying situations encountered along the way by the Christian pilgrim; interwoven throughout are quotations and passages directly from the Bible. It is as relevant today as it was when first published over three hundred years ago.

The allegory is in the form of a dream in which Bunyan sees the main character, Christian, (The

Pilgrim) with a great burden on his back reading a book. It is in this book, the word of God, that Christian learns of dreadful consequences if he is not delivered from the guilt and power of his sin and seeks to escape from destruction.

The book he reads causes him to cry out for help. A man named Evangelist encourages him and sets him in the right direction, and the pilgrim turns to flee from the City of Destruction, having failed to persuade his wife and family to come away with him. Many Christians at the time it was first written, and since, would identify with this dramatic storyline in Bunyan's masterpiece and fully appreciate the underlying principles in the Christian life that it portrays.

As the story unfolds it is not long before Pilgrim falls into the miry Slough of Despond, and here as he flounders and struggles, he is aided and brought out by a man named Help. The pilgrim continues his journey after passing through a little Wicket Gate pointed out to him by Evangelist,

which opens onto a straight and narrow path, which will lead him in the end to the Celestial City. Soon however, he is receiving sound guidance and encouragement at the Interpreter's House. After leaving the Interpreter he eventually comes to a hilly place where he sees a Cross and beneath this cross he feels his burden fall from off his back and roll away into an open grave to be seen no more.

Travelling on, Christian finds rest at the House Beautiful, where ladies named Discretion, Prudence, Piety and Charity talk with him over dinner. He leaves the hospitality of this opulent place the following morning after a night's sleep in a room called Peace.

The pilgrim continues on through varied situations such as the Valley of Humiliation, the Valley of the Shadow of Death, Vanity Fair where he narrowly escapes death, the Delectable Mountains with their gardens and orchards, vineyards and fountains from which the pilgrim can see the country of Beulah and the Celestial City.

On this journey he meets various allegorical characters, each one displaying their own distinct characteristics. Among these are Mr Worldly Wiseman, who sounds convincing but is actually trying to persuade him to stray from the right path.

Another is Faithful, who accompanies Christian on his way but is stoned to death in Vanity Fair, and Hopeful, who is a good companion on the pilgrimage. Some harrowing encounters are made on the journey including, Giant Despair, who has a wife named Gloom. He captures Christian and locks him up in the stronghold of Doubting Castle. Another character that Christian encounters is Judge Hategood at Vanity Fair, who clearly reflects Kelynge, the judge who Bunyan himself faced at the Bedford Assize in 1660. Then there is the foul fiend Apollyon, who breathes fire, has dragon's wings and a mouth like a lion, and stares at Christian with a most horrible look. Yet as Christian fights and defends himself from this mighty attacker, the language and visionary drama that Bunyan uses from Scripture to describe Christian's fight with the devil is incredibly vivid.

The storyline in the first part of *The Pilgrim's Progress* concludes as Christian safely passes through the River of Death where on the other side, to the sound of heavenly music Christian and Hopeful enter into the Celestial City. Finally we read, 'I awoke and behold it was a dream.'

The second part of *The*

Above: The brass
plaque found on the
wall of the northern
end of the east
parapet of the town
bridge

Left: A collection of
differing editions of
The Pilgrim's Progress

Pilgrim's Progress, Bunyan's last
major publication, was written in
1685. It centres on the pilgrimage
of Christian's wife Christiana, and
her children, who he had left
behind when he left the City of
Destruction. Following a dream,
and with the company of her
neighbour, Mercy, they set out
together on a similar pilgrimage.
Despite objections and difficulties,
they are helped by Great-heart,
who sees off Giant Despair and
other enemies. Mr Honest, Mr
Despondency and his daughter
Much-Afraid, Mr Steadfast and
Mr Valiant-for-truth are all
encountered before they too reach
their desired destination: 'So she

went and called, and entered in at
the gate with all the ceremonies of
joy that her husband Christian had
done before her.'

This work was written in a
more mature style than the first
part. It is in this section of *The
Pilgrim's Progress* that the words
of the pilgrim's poem: '*Who
would true valour see*', appear.
The original wording of Bunyan
has since been altered in some
hymnbooks giving us the well-
known hymn: '*He who would
valiant be*'. Today it is sung in
churches worldwide to its equally
famous tune, *Monks Gate*,
composed from an English
traditional melody by Ralph
Vaughan Williams.

The Pilgrim's Progress was an
instant success. Within ten years
of the first publication it passed
through ten editions, totalling a
remarkable one hundred thousand
copies. It was published in several
other European languages even
before Bunyan's death. The
story is admired as an
international classic, and has
been published in over two
hundred languages
throughout the world since it
first appeared. Although his
writings were very popular,
Bunyan earned little income
from the sale of his books,
and at his death, his estate
valued only approximately
fifty pounds!

Two hundred years later it
was claimed, with only a slight
exaggeration, that every
household in England possessed
two books, the Bible and a
copy of *The Pilgrim's
Progress*.

WEST END
*BAPTIST MEETING
HOUSE*

GREAT OUSE

STEVINGTON
VILLAGE
CROSS

STEVINGTON

WINDMILL

JOHN BUNYAN TRAIL

TO NORTHAMPTON

A 428 (T)

TO BEDFORD
(4 MILES)

BROMHAM

SCALE = 1 MILE

**PRESENT DAY SITES
DEPICTED IN *THE
PILGRIM'S PROGRESS***

It is still possible to
find places and
sites around
Bedfordshire that
may have been in
Bunyan's mind when
he wrote his famous
allegory. It must be
stressed, however,
that Bunyan did
not detail places
himself and the list
shown is purely
speculative.

Above: *North west door, Elstow parish church*

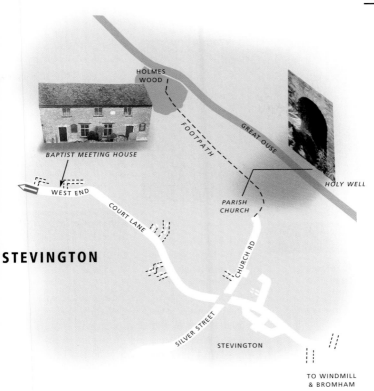

SCALE = 1/2 MILE

Beelzebub's Castle and the Wicket Gate

OS Grid reference TL 049475

'A little distance from this gate there is erected a strong castle'

Standing in front of the unused old wooden door in the north corner at the west end of Elstow Abbey church, you are beneath the high bell tower which stands isolated from the church to your left. This place may have been in Bunyan's mind when he portrayed them in the early part of *The Pilgrim's Progress.*

By Car: Elstow is 3 kilometres (2 miles) from Bedford town centre via the A6 (Luton). Follow the brown directional road signs in Elstow for the Moot Hall on the village green. Ample car parking is available at the west end of the church or at the Moot Hall during opening hours. The keys to the church are available from the Vicarage or 209, Church End, (in the row of cottages beyond the church car park) at reasonable times.

Public transport: Bus service No 143/144 Bedford Bus Station Bay 7 to Elstow Red Lion (not Sundays).

housing estate is reached. Cross the stream at the road bridge that connects two residential housing areas to reach the subway beyond, that passes under the Bedford by-pass dual carriageway. (See the information on pages 19-20).

The Slough of Despond

OS Grid reference TL 057475

'. . they drew near to a very miry slough...The name of this slough was Despond'.

Several sites in Bedfordshire could lay claim to this description as marshes and boggy patches were more prevalent in the 17th century. An area strongly meeting this description is between Elstow and Bunyan's birthplace at Harrowden. Much of the marshy ground here has been drained and houses have been built in the vicinity in recent years. It is still possible to walk from Elstow village alongside the brook to Harrowden, a distance of about 2.5 kilometres (1—2 miles). The footpath commences at the southern end of the High

Street, to the left of the road bridge that crosses over the brook. Keep the brook to your right throughout this walk. After passing the main entrance to Abbey School, remains of marshes will be seen on the right beyond the far bank of the stream, at the point where the school playing fields end. To extend your walk to the site of Bunyan's birthplace at Harrowden, follow the footpath across the meadows. In Bunyan's time these would have been open marshes. Eventually a

The Interpreter's House

OS Grid reference TL 052492

'Then he went on till he came at the house of the Interpreter.'

The home of Mr John Gifford whose ministry was most helpful to Bunyan at the time of his conversion stands prominently on the east side of St. John's Street, Bedford, next to the church where the dissenters in the area first

Top: *Elstow Brook*

Above: *St. John's Rectory—'The Interpreter's House'*

met for worship in 1650. Today the house is the Bedfordshire headquarters of the St. John Ambulance Service. The old rectory has one room depicting Bunyan's time, open to the public by appointment. ☎ 01234 216200.

The church of St. John was extensively restored in 1869-70. It consists of a chancel, nave, west porch and a west tower containing one bell. Below a figurine of a little lamb on the west wall of the tower are the words in Latin, 'Ecce Agnus Dei', ('Behold the Lamb of God'), the words of John the Baptist in John 1:29.

The Cross and the Sepulchre

OS map reference SP 989533

'. .I saw in my dream, that just as Christian came up with the Cross, his burden loosed . . and fell off his back and began to tumble, . . till it came to the mouth of the sepulchre, where I saw it no more. .'

Above: *Stevington Cross dates from medieval times*

T he village of Stevington lies 10 kilometres (6 miles) north east of Bedford. There is conjecture that this site was in Bunyan's mind when he wrote *The Pilgrim's Progress*. In the heart of the village at a crossroads is an imposing 14th century cross, a grey stone slender column raised upon high steps, with a square canopied head. Church Road leads down the hill from the crossroads, past quaint stone cottages towards the village church of St. Mary the Virgin. Car parking is possible here before the church gates (please keep the gateway clear). On foot, follow the track that descends to the right of the church gate, after approximately 50 metres a footpath bears off to the left (it is often damp underfoot here and may be covered in undergrowth during summer months). After another 50 metres on the left hand side, at the foot of the high churchyard wall is a man-made arch covering an open spring, known as 'The Holy Well', which bubbles up from beneath the church grounds. It is said the spring never freezes over or dries up! Thousands of pilgrims came to visit the well during the Middle Ages to partake of the water, which was thought to contain healing powers!

Any connection the cross and the well have with Bunyan and *The Pilgrim's Progress* may be imaginative, yet beyond the spring, the footpath continues across the meadows to the River Great Ouse, less than a kilometre away. Here, John would sometimes preach in the cover of the beech trees and undergrowth which lined the banks of the river, and the early Baptists from Stevington would baptise their converts in the secrecy of this secluded spot, known as 'Holmes Wood'. The Independent church in Stevington was founded in 1655 and a meeting house, built in 1720, stands at the north end of the village beyond Meeting Farm on the road to Pavenham.

Picture: *The 'Holy Well', below Stevington church*

Stevington by car:
Leave Bedford via the A428 (Northampton) road. After passing Bromham turn right off the A428 at the sign for Stevington.

Stevington by public transport:
The No 134 bus service from Bedford bus station runs at regular intervals daily. (☎ 0870 608 2 608 for Travel Line details) *The village area is suitable for wheelchairs although beyond the church the footpath becomes difficult and uneven.*

Stevington Windmill

To the south of the village on the road to Bromham, an impressive postmill built in the 18th century is the only complete windmill left in Bedfordshire. Open all year 10am to 7pm (or dusk, if sooner) Keys available from the pubs in Stevington (£5 returnable deposit). An adult must accompany children. ☎ 01234 824330

(There is a 17th century restored watermill set on the banks of the River Ouse at Bromham.

Refreshments are served overlooking the river. Flour milling and baking takes place regularly. Open Mar to Oct, Wed to Sat 1pm –5pm. Bank holidays 10.30 to 5pm. ☎ 01234 824330 for further details.)

Above: Houghton House

The Hill Difficulty

OS map reference TL 033389

'..they all went on till they came to the foot of the hill Difficulty,'

North of the Georgian town of Ampthill is the Greensands Ridge, part of the Chiltern range of hills. Driving south from Bedford on the B530 for 10 kilometres (6 miles), the mid Bedfordshire town of Ampthill is entered by ascending this hill range (just beyond the point where a 40 MPH speed restriction zone is entered). In the mid 17th century, this would have been a steep and difficult climb on a dirt track; progress would have been slow and dangerous. In *The Pilgrim's Progress*, Bunyan describes it as steep and high, causing Christian to ascend it upon his hands and knees.

Palace Beautiful

OS map reference TL 039395

' ...there was a very stately palace before him, the name of which was Beautiful,'

On the B530 at the top of Ampthill hill is the roadway to the left leading to Houghton House (Follow the brown direction road sign). A visitor's car park is at the end of this roadway (before the cattle grid). There is then a half-mile walk past farm cottages to the ruin of the house, which is now in the care of English Heritage.

This former Jacobean-hunting lodge gives commanding views over the Marston Vale that stretches out to the north and it would certainly have been the most noble and stately building in the area during the mid-17th century. Built c.1615 for Mary, Countess of Pembroke, it is believed that Bunyan would have visited the house as a tinker to mend pots and pans, and knew its interior. Originally, the house, built in red brick, was three storeys high, with square towers at each corner. The main staircase in the Swan Hotel, Bedford is reputed to have come from the house following its partial demolition during the 18th century.

On a clear day, looking south from the visitor's car park it is possible to see the Chiltern Hills; these may have been in Bunyan's mind as the Delectable Mountains, pointed out to Christian in *The Pilgrim's Progress* the morning he left the Palace Beautiful.

Public transport:
Service 142/143/144. Bedford Bus station Bay 7 to Ampthill Town centre. Houghton House is 1 mile north of the town centre via Bedford Street. The site is not suitable for wheelchair access.

Ampthill

The ancient market town of Ampthill has association with Henry VIII who often visited the area for country sports, staying at the 15th century castle that once stood in Ampthill Park. Most of his wives stayed in the castle, including his first wife, Catherine of Aragon who lived here from 1531 until divorced in 1533. The castle fell into disrepair during the reign of Elizabeth I, but a cross (erected in 1770), known as Katherine's Cross, stands on the site.

The present house in the park was built 1686-88 for the Dowager Countess of Ailesbury (Aylesbury) and Elgin, by architect-mason Robert Grumbold of Cambridge. It was sold to the first Lord Ashburnham in 1690. More recently it was a Cheshire Home, for people with physical disabilities, but is now divided into several private apartments.

Ampthill boasts many Georgian listed buildings built along four main streets that meet at the Market Square. The Square itself is dominated by a clock tower originally part of the old Moot Hall of 1852. An obelisk pump is in the Square and was at one time a major water supply for the town. The parish church on the edge of open hill-country east of the town, is dedicated to St. Andrew and was built of ironstone in the 14th century in Perpendicular Gothic style. Four brasses include one to Sir Nicholas Harvey 1532 who attended Queen Catherine, and a marble memorial commemorating the life of Colonel Richard Nicolls—the man responsible for giving New York its name, can be found in the church.

The town centre car park off Bedford Street is a useful point for setting out on numerous walks around the town and the woodlands to the west of the town and beyond.

Railway Station: Flitwick Thameslink 3.5 kilometres (2 Miles).

The Valley of the Shadow of Death

OS Grid reference TL 014385

'Now this valley was a very solitary place..'

West of Ampthill, nestled in a tree-lined gorge in the northern edge of the Chiltern Hills that form the Greensand Ridge in mid-Bedfordshire, lies the tiny village of Millbrook. The church of St. Michael and All Angels dominates the village on the hill above where on a clear day it is said The Wash, beyond the Fenlands of East Anglia, can be seen from the tower.

Bunyan would have travelled through this gorge on journeys south from Bedford. As he relates in *The Pilgrim's Progress,* the pathway was dark and narrow, more overpowering and striking probably than it is now. However there is still a sense that this could be the site of Bunyan's valley as you pass through the village in the gloom of the overhanging trees.

By Car: Millbrook is one mile west of Ampthill off the A507 road to Woburn. There is a small car park to the north of the village on the road to Marston

Moretaine, from where walks into the village and the surrounding countryside can be made.

By Public Transport: A train service runs hourly from Bedford station to Millbrook on the Marston Vale railway line (except Sundays). Millbrook station is 1.5 kilometres (1 mile) north of the village. ☎ 08457 484 950

The Delectable Mountains

'These mountains are Immanuel's land'

The Chiltern Hills, just north of Luton, although not high in comparison to some parts of the country, are nevertheless quite imposing. To someone like Bunyan who in the 17th century would not have travelled widely throughout the British Isles and seen high peaks, the Chiltern Range above Barton-le-Clay would have appeared mountainous. Bunyan was familiar with the hills between Dunstable and Hitchin, where he preached on many occasions, often in secret locations.

Today several walks on these hills are available to walkers. Neither of these sites detailed below are suitable for wheelchair access.

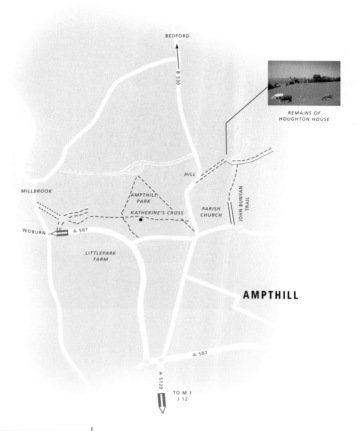

BEDFORD

B 530

REMAINS OF
HOUGHTON HOUSE

HILL

MILLBROOK

AMPTHILD
PARK

KATHERINE'S CROSS

PARISH
CHURCH

JOHN BUNYAN TRAIL

WOBURN — A 507

LITTLEPARK
FARM

AMPTHILL

A 507

A 5120

TO M 1
J 12

SCALE = 1 MILE

Picture: *Sharpenhoe Hills 'The Delectable Mountains'*

Sharpenhoe Clappers

**OS Grid reference
TL 066296**

By Car from Bedford:

Drive south on the A6 for 21 kilometres (13 miles). Leave A6 at the roundabout north of Barton-le-Clay and enter the village on the B655. At a roundabout in the centre of village, turn right on

Above: *Christian talking with Simple, Sloth and Presumption (from the Meeting, Bedford doors)*

unclassified road for Sharpenhoe. After approx. 1.5 kilometres (1 mile) turn left in the centre of Sharpenhoe, at the Lynmore Public House, for Sharpenhoe Clappers. The car park for walks to Sharpenhoe Clappers is after 1.5 kilometres (1 mile) on the left. The word 'clappers' means 'rabbit warren'.

Sundon Hills Country Park

OS Grid reference TL 048285

By car from Bedford:

Drive south on the A6 for 21 kilometres (13 miles). Leave the A6 at the roundabout north of

Barton-le Clay and enter the village on the B655. At a roundabout in centre of the village, turn right on an unclassified road for Sharpenhoe and Harlington. After five kilometres (3 miles), as you enter the village of Harlington, good views of

the 'Delectable Mountains' can be seen to the left. At the crossroads in the centre of Harlington, beyond the village church, turn left for Upper Sundon. After approx. 2.5 kilometres (1–2 miles) the car park for Sundon Hills Country Park is on the left.

Bronze Doors

The doors of the Bunyan Meeting Church are copper on bronze, and were given to the Church in 1876 by Hastings, 9th Duke of Bedford. They are modelled on the Baptistry Doors at Florence, and are the work of sculptor Frederick Thrupp. (See page 55 for more details).

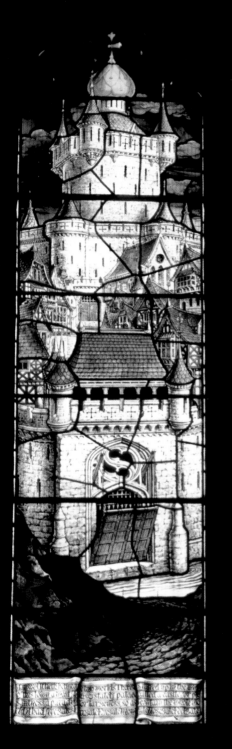

⑦ From prisoner to pastor

Bunyan's life was full of drama and adventure, but it is the small and personal things, like the flute he made in prison and the chair he used as pastor of the Elstow congregation, that remind us of his life and important legacy

Between 1661 and 1663 Bunyan made several further attempts to regain his freedom from custody but on each occasion his plea for clemency was unsuccessful, mainly due to the efforts locally of Paul Cobb to keep Bunyan in prison. As the months went by the possibility of an early release for Bunyan seemed to fade.

His prison life fell into a regular pattern. He would sit for hours in his cell reading either the Bible or the only other book he possessed there, *Foxe's Book of Martyrs*, interspersed with praying and writing. At other times he would actively join in discussions with other Independent church inmates and the Quakers with whom sometimes the debate would become quite a heated affair.

There is a story that Bunyan also occupied himself by secretly making a flute out of one of the legs of his prison stool. After carefully hollowing out the wood he used the flame of his candle to make the holes in the barrel needed to play the instrument. When the inquisitive gaoler came to investigate the music sounding from the cell, Bunyan would quickly return the wooden flute to its original use beneath the stool! The flute, along with a small violin he made from thin iron plate years earlier at Elstow, and inscribed, 'John Bunyan, Helstow', can be seen today in the Bunyan Museum, Bedford.

Bunyan's treatment during his confinement varied as different prison authorities came and went. It is evident that on some occasions Bunyan was even allowed to leave the gaol for short periods at a time and he took full

Left: *The Holy War: section of a a stained glass window at Elstow Parish Church*

Above: *Model statuette of Bunyan by Boehm, 1875*

advantage of this to preach and visit Christian friends. He tells us: 'I had by my gaoler some liberty granted to me, more than at the first.' The minute book of the Bedford Independent church records that on 28 August 1661 'brother Bunyan' was instructed to visit two church members for non-attendance at meetings. Other similar entries were to appear at a later date and it is obvious that John was held in high regard for his pastoral care and skills.

The Clarendon Code

In early 1662 an Act of Uniformity was passed. Several laws passed by the new Parliament at that time became known as the Clarendon Code after the Earl of Clarendon, Edward Hyde, Charles II's chief minister of state. This particular act meant that every clergyman and minister of religion must, within three months, accept unreservedly the *Book of Common Prayer* and ordination by a bishop. In the event over two thousand clergy refused and were therefore ejected from their churches. More was to follow, because in 1664 a new Conventicle Act became law and lasted for three years. This forbad all informal religious meetings except those in the established church, and any lawbreaker faced a five-pound fine or a three-month prison sentence. Added to this, during October 1665, the Great Plague was sweeping across London, and other major cities and towns. Parliament moved to Oxford in an effort to avoid it and from there issued the Five Mile Act, which forbad ejected 'non-conformist' ministers from visiting places where they had previously held office or of living within five miles of any major town. This act made it very difficult for many independent ministers and teachers to earn a living, and during the next three years several hundred men and

---

Foxe's Book of Martyrs

Until Bunyan wrote *The Pilgrim's Progress* there were few major books in print in England apart from the Bible, the works of Shakespeare and John Foxe's *Book of Martyrs*, or to give it its full puritanical title: *Acts and Monuments of these Latter and Perilous Days, touching the church, from the year of our Lord a*

thousand to the time now present.

John Foxe (pictured) was born in 1516 in Boston, Lincolnshire and was educated at Oxford from 1539 to 1545. He became a fellow at Magdalen College, specialising in church history. It appears, however, that because of his extreme Protestant sentiments he was eventually expelled from the college. During the reign of the Roman Catholic, Queen Mary, he fled to the continent

to avoid persecution, but while in exile he began work on the *Book of Martyrs*, which was published in Basel during 1559 in Latin. That year Elizabeth came to the

women were to be arrested whilst they attended meetings. Prisons throughout the country, including Bedford, were full to overcrowding with dissenters and they must have become very uncomfortable places.

The Bedford Independent church book was locked away for safe keeping between 1664 and 1668 as the church was constantly harassed and watched by the

Above: Wooden flute and a metal violin—both reputed to have been made by Bunyan, and exhibited in the Bunyan Museum, Bedford

throne and John Foxe returned to England. He was ordained in 1560 and became a prebendary at Salisbury cathedral in 1563, the same year that the *Book of Martyrs* was first published in English.

In 1570, Queen Elizabeth ordered that a copy of the *Book of Martyrs* be placed in the common halls of archbishops and bishops as well as colleges and chapels throughout the kingdom.

In his book, Foxe gave a detailed history of early English Protestant martyrs highlighting the power of faith. It is perhaps understandable that as a 'best seller', it left a deep impression and contributed to the Protestant identity in England during the 16th and 17th century, influencing several contemporary writers including John Bunyan.

All who could read the book in those days learnt the full horrors of atrocities

meted out to Protestant reformers. Illiterate people saw the crude, yet sensational woodcut illustrations it contained of various instruments used in torture, the rack, the gridiron, boiling oil, as well as believers burning at the stake amid faggots and flames.

Numerous editions of the *Book of Martyrs* have appeared since the first publication, and it is still in print today.

Pictured: Bunyan's statue, Bedford. Erected in 1874—a gift to the town from the Duke of Bedford

authorities. However, its elders and members maintained a remarkable spirit of unity and prayer and the spiritual life of the church flourished through this long and dangerous decade.

Dramatic Times

1666 was the year in which a fire began in a little baker's shop in Pudding Lane, near London Bridge, in London in the early hours of 2 September. It developed quickly and spread through many dwellings and business places that were in the heart of the city. Samuel Pepys, the famous 17th century diarist, (who incidentally, visited Bedford in 1668) gave a vivid description of the fire in his writings.

During the summer of 1668 Bunyan was released from prison. He was able to return home to his family who were fast growing up, able to resume his duties in the church, and again able to preach the doctrines of Scriptures that he loved. However, this freedom was short-lived, and within weeks he was re-arrested. The laws that had lapsed allowing John his short period of freedom were once again enforced and he returned to Bedford Gaol. A future close friend of Bunyan, Charles Doe, recorded later that 'a little after his release they took him again at a meeting, and put him in the same gaol, where he lay six years more.' Yet another blow for Bunyan that year was the death, at eighteen, of his dear blind daughter, Mary.

Little is known of the events surrounding his re-arrest and time back in prison. It was doubtless a

Above: Bunyan Meeting Free Church Bedford. Built in 1850 on the site of the original barn used by Bunyan's congregation from 1662

similar routine for John, but only two books were produced during the next six years. The relative silence may be for many reasons; one might have been that Bunyan was working on his greatest literary work, *The Pilgrim's Progress*—which was not finally published until 1678.

The Act of Indulgence

National affairs around 1670 were in jeopardy. Lord Clarendon had been dismissed as Lord Chancellor and the King's policies altered erratically. Money was in short supply and Charles would spend irrationally and often before funds were raised. The King also entered into closer international ties with France, which would weaken him further.

He signed the Treaty of Dover in which he pledged to acknowledge himself as Roman Catholic and in return received £200,000 a year from Louis XIV (a vast sum at the time) with the offer of French troops to repress any possible Protestant uprisings. To encourage this diplomacy at home, the King issued a Declaration of Indulgence on 15 March 1672, in an effort to quietly change the government's official religious policy in order to benefit Roman Catholics; this ironically had the effect of benefitting Nonconformists and Quakers as well.

Thousands were given back their freedom of conscience, including John Bunyan of Bedford and several of his close

Above: Pastor Bunyan's chair. Used by John Bunyan during his ministry at Bedford 1672-1688

Below: Bunyan Meeting Church founded in 1650. The present building was built in 1850 at a cost of £3,400

acquaintances. John, although only forty-three, stepped out of prison, physically showing the signs of his twelve-year ordeal. On 9 May 1672, he received a licence to teach under the Declaration of Indulgence and gained the opportunity and official right to 'call the people together for prayer.' His wife Elizabeth, who had given birth to a girl, Sarah in 1668, was pregnant again and in November 1672, Joseph was born and christened in St. Cuthbert's church.

The Mill Lane Church

Following the death of John Burton in 1660, the church experienced a time without a pastor. Various solutions to this were sought. Yet according to the church record of October 1663, Samuel Fenne (who had himself just been released from prison) and John Whitehead, both

Above: The Old Meeting House, Bedford in use from 1707 until 1850

members of the fellowship, were given joint responsibly for pastoring the congregation. However, in the autumn of 1671 the Bedford Independent church met secretly in the nearby village of Haynes to consider their choice of a new pastor. After procrastinations and long meetings the Church minute book records that on 21 January 1672, John Bunyan was appointed as Pastor, 'with joynt consent.' This was just weeks before his eventual release from prison. He was to be the fifth pastor of the Bedford Meeting.

The church now had another pastor but following its eviction from St. John's church in 1660, it was still without a place of worship in which to meet. In May 1672, a member of the congregation purchased from Justice Crompton of Elstow an orchard and barn in Mill Lane, near to the church of St. Cuthbert's. The barn was then sold to the church for £50, licensed for preaching and converted for use as a place of worship. It was a convenient spot, just two minutes walk from the new pastor's home. An indenture conveying the orchard and barn to its new owner, Josias Ruffhead, is in the Bunyan Museum. Although by the standards of the day it was a commodious meetinghouse, on the opening day, such was the popularity now of John Bunyan, that a great crowd gathered and the meeting was reconvened in the open air.

The converted barn served the church well for thirty-five years until it was replaced by a three gabled structure known as the 'Old Meeting' in 1707. It seated 700 people and although altered several times over the ensuing years the congregation met in it until the present Bunyan Meeting church was built in 1850 at a cost of £3,400.

As for John Bunyan, he resumed his preaching not only in Bedford but surrounding towns, villages and counties where he gained the affectionate title of 'bishop Bunyan'.

8 The end of the pilgrimage

In 1688 a great preacher and writer died. To visit the sites
associated with Bunyan's life and stand by his tomb in
Bunhill Fields in the heart of busy and noisy London, more
than three hundred years later, is a reminder of the power of
his life and work that spread across the world

Bunyan's father, Thomas,
died at Harrowden in 1676
at the age of 74. He was
buried in the churchyard at Elstow
on the 7th February, yet it is
unclear whether John was present
at his father's burial as it took
place twelve months before John's
final release from prison. Thomas
had continued to live at their
family home following John's
hasty departure in 1644 for
military service. According to
records, each of his surviving
children received one shilling (five
pence) and the remainder of his
few belongings went to his wife,
Anne. Whether or not Thomas
had shown any support for his son
during those long years of
imprisonment and suffering for
conscience's sake is not known,
but he may have come to John's
way of thinking because at his
death he committed his soul into
the care of Almighty God, hoping
to receive pardon through the

death of Jesus Christ, 'his only
Saviour and Redeemer'.

John Bunyan was finally
released from prison in 1677. He
was now 49 years of age and he
was to live for just over ten more
years. These were years that he
used to the full and it could be said
they were years of triumph. His
periods of imprisonment, his
writings and his powerful
preaching had made him a

*Opposite page: The Belfry of St John's Church, Bedford. It was in this
church that Bunyan sat under the teaching of John Gifford at the time of
his conversion*

*Above: Bunyan on horseback, from a 17th century print—one of three held
at the Bunyan Museum in Bedford*

popular man far beyond Bedford.

John, now carrying in his pocket his licence to preach and teach, immediately responded to the many requests from Nonconformist congregations and others, to preach in different parts of the country, particularly London, which he endeavoured to visit at least once a year. He would arrange preaching tours that meant him being away from home for days, even weeks at a time. One example of this is his affinity with the Independent church at Bocking near Braintree in Essex. He is said to have stayed on several occasions at the homes of the leaders of the Bocking Independent Meeting, reputed to be one of the earliest Nonconformist groups in England with links as far back as 1550. John would preach in the large barn on a farm at Bocking End or in the Town Square outside the White Hart Inn, which still stands today, to hundreds of Nonconformists who would eagerly gather from all over Essex to hear him. It is believed locally that work on a book which may have been *The Life and Death of Mr Badman* or *The Holy War* was undertaken in a quiet upstairs room on the farm that was made available by his local friends.

He would travel on his long distance trips on horseback over roads that were full of potholes and mud, and as he travelled, Bunyan would notice a change in the countryside from that which he knew earlier in his life. Large areas of thick woodland were being removed as trees were felled for much needed timber to build ever bigger ships for the growing navy as well for house building as towns and villages began to develop and expand into rural areas. Heath and moorland was also slowly being cultivated for farmland. During the reign of

Dr John Owen

John Owen, who was probably the most powerful of the Puritan theologians, was born in 1616 at Stadhampton, Oxfordshire, where his father was village rector. At the age of twelve he entered Queen's college, Oxford, and he gained a BA in 1632 followed by an MA in 1635. He studied diligently, allowing himself only four hours sleep, and damaged his health permanently by this arduous regime.

In 1642 Owen was appointed Rector of Fordham, Essex. However, four years later, at the age of thirty he moved to nearby Coggeshall where he came out in favour of Congregational autonomy in church government. After preaching a notable sermon before Parliament in 1646, he began a friendship with Oliver Cromwell, and generally supported his policies. Following the execution of King Charles I in January 1649, Owen accompanied Cromwell as a chaplain on his military ventures to Ireland and Scotland between 1649-50. Owen went back to Coggeshall in 1651 but the following March, Cromwell appointed him Vice Chancellor at Oxford, a post he held

Charles II, it became popular for wealthy landowners to plant avenues of trees along formal carriage driveways, which further changed the appearance of the English countryside.

Journeys in those days were not without dangers, for robbers and highwaymen were a hazard to any traveller. The twisted wooden frame that stands today on the grass verge at Caxton Gibbet, just south of the A428/A1198 roundabout, 13 kilometres (8 miles) west of Cambridge, still bears witness to the age when these common criminals were hung by the neck and their bodies left hanging on chains for their crimes against unsuspecting travellers. Travel fatigue was another difficulty. Journeys that are now taken for granted, such as Bedford to London in under an hour by train, could have taken well over a day in the late 1600s.

John would sometimes stop off

Above: Stevington Baptist Meeting

on his journeys south to London and preach in remote villages in Hertfordshire. In Wainwood, a pretty bluebell wood just north of the picturesque village of Preston, near Hitchin, is a natural looking amphitheatre, probably excavated in ancient times amongst the trees, where he would preach to those assembled on the secret slopes of

until 1657. His university conferred the honour of Doctor of Divinity upon him in December 1652.

Dr Owen opposed plans to offer the English crown to Cromwell and avoided participation in Cromwell's installation in the office of Lord Protector in 1653. He abandoned politics on the restoration of the monarchy in 1660, when the House of Commons removed him from his position as dean of Christ

Church, Oxford.

During his life he issued more than eighty different publications, many of them of great size. Among these are several notable studies on the doctrine of the Holy Spirit, and defences of Nonconformist, or Puritan, views. He accepted his final pastorate in 1673 at a church in Leadenhall Street, London.

There is evidence that Dr Owen used his great

influence and reputation on Bunyan's behalf. In June 1677 he approached the Bishop of Lincoln, Dr Thomas Barlow, to help secure Bunyan's release from his second imprisonment.

Owen died on 23 August 1683, in Ealing at the age of 67, and was buried in Bunhill Fields, London, on 4 September, almost five years to the day before John Bunyan was interred in the same cemetery.

*Below: The remains of
the cottage at Coleman
Green where Bunyan
reputedly lodged and
preached in the garden*

*Opposite: Coleman
Green, Hertfordshire*

the dell. It can still be clearly seen
today. At other times Bunyan
would call at a small hamlet near
Wheathampstead, known today as
Coleman Green. Today, the
chimney-stack is all that remains
of the cottage that is reputedly
where Bunyan lodged occasionally
and preached in the adjoining
garden. The area is a pleasant site
to visit; with walks into the nearby
woods. Opposite the old cottage
stands a public house named after
the one time famous visitor.

London preaching

Bunyan was well received by the
congregations he preached to in
London, with crowds flocking to
hear him. Apart from meeting
houses, he would preach in many
of the halls where nonconformists
worshipped in those days
following the great fire of 1666.
Pinners' Hall, Gilders' Hall and
Salters' Hall were among them. A
friend of Bunyan at the time,
Charles Doe, was a comb maker
and lived in Southwark where
Shakespeare's now famous
reconstructed Globe theatre
stands, just south of the River
Thames; he recorded how
enthusiastic people were to hear
Bunyan preach: 'When Mr Bunyan
preached in London, if there was
but one day's notice given, there
would be more people come
together to hear him preach than
the meeting house would hold.
I have seen to hear him preach, by
my computation, about twelve
hundred at a morning lecture by
seven o'clock on a working day in
the dark wintertime. I also
computed about three thousand
that came to him on the Lord's

Day (Sunday) at London, at a town's end's meeting house, so that half were fain to go back again for want of room, and then himself was fain at the back door to be pulled almost over people to get upstairs to his pulpit.' Mr Doe held John in such affection that following the preacher's death he endeavoured to find and publish Bunyan's unpublished manuscripts.

Bunyan had other friends in London including Dr John Owen, the Puritan Vice-Chancellor of Oxford University who on one occasion was asked by King Charles II why he went so often to hear John Bunyan preach? Dr Owen favourably replied, 'I would happily exchange all my learning for the ability to preach Christ as the tinker of Bedford does.' During the early 1680s Dr Owen was a minister in the city of London where Bunyan would preach occasionally at his church.

Twenty years after his succession to the throne, Charles II was beginning to lose his popularity. He often acted without the consent of Parliament, and his allegiance towards Roman Catholics was a topic for debate and concern. Once again the fear of Civil War was threatening. John Bunyan wrote at the time: 'Our days indeed had been days of trouble…we began to fear cutting of throats, of being burned in our beds, and of seeing our children dashed in pieces before our faces.' John continued his writing. Could it have been the turmoil that surrounded him which prompted his writing of *The Holy War*, published in 1682? Charles II died in 1685 and his brother James II, a confessed Roman Catholic, succeeded him.

During the difficult years of the mid 1680s the church was again persecuted and meetings were often held in secret places for fear

Above: Baptist Meeting Gamlingay today

of trouble and imprisonment. Bunyan felt that at any time and without warning he might be arrested again. He decided to draw up a 'Deed of Gift' so that should anything happen to him, his wife would be secure. Four church members at Bedford witnessed the deed, written on 23 December 1685, in John's own handwriting. It began: 'To all people to whom this present writing shall come, I, John Bunyan of the parish of St. Cuthberts, in the town of Bedford, brazier, send greeting. Know ye that I, the said John Bunyan, as well for and in consideration of the natural affection and love which I have and bear unto my well-beloved wife, Elizabeth, as also for divers other good causes and considerations me at this present especially moving, have given and granted ... all and singular my goods, chattels, debts, ready money, plate, rings, household stuff, apparel, utensils, brass, pewter, bedding, and all other my substance whatsoever ...'

The document, though not a will, would ensure that his possessions could not be seized if he were arrested or fined for any reason. So secretly was it hidden however, that Elizabeth did not appear to know of its existence because it was only discovered—hidden between bricks in the chimney—when his house was demolished in 1838, one hundred and fifty years after his death. It is now in the possession of the Bunyan museum in Bedford.

Behind Bunyan's back
Another difficulty that Bunyan had to contend with occasionally was slander. One interesting story that survives illustrates this clearly. It involved Agnes Beaumont, a young woman who joined the

Bunyan meeting church at Gamlingay, just over the Cambridgeshire border, soon after Bunyan became pastor at Bedford. She lived with her widowed father in a little farm cottage at Edworth, a small village between Biggleswade and Baldock.

Originally Agnes had attended meetings with her father but due to malicious gossip he became convinced that Bunyan and his church were dangerous. From then on Agnes often found great difficulty attending meetings without upsetting her father. On one occasion she was particularly anxious to be at a meeting at Gamlingay and was pleased that her father reluctantly agreed she could attend. It was arranged that a pastor from Hitchin, John Wilson, who passed through Edworth would call for her. Agnes was to ride the seven miles across the Bedfordshire countryside behind him on horseback. The man failed to appear however. As it was the depth of winter the mud and wintery conditions made it almost impossible for Agnes to walk and her brother's horse was not available either. Poor Agnes was beginning to fear that she would be disappointed, when unexpectedly Mr Bunyan rode by on his way to the same meeting.

Bunyan refused to take Agnes at first for fear of upsetting her father yet, reluctantly, he agreed after her brother pleaded on her behalf. Their father realised what was happening soon after the two of them set off into the distance. Furiously he hurried to cut them off at a point along the road, but missed them. Agnes felt proud to be behind Mr Bunyan as they journeyed in silence. She was only three years older than his daughter, Mary, and Bunyan was well aware of the scandal that this situation could bring for him. After the meeting Bunyan returned home directly to Bedford. A young woman who had also attended the meeting from a neighbouring village agreed to take Agnes for part of the return journey on horseback; however, Agnes was forced to walk the last past of the journey. When she eventually arrived home she discovered her angry father had locked her out of the cottage, and she spent a cold night in an adjacent barn. Tales did surround the occasion and caused commotion in the locality for a time. After her death in 1720 Agnes was buried in the graveyard of John Wilson's Tilehouse Street chapel, Hitchin, and a commemorative tablet was erected on the rear wall of the building. Bunyan refers to the slander that related to him on occasions in later editions of *Grace Abounding:* '…it belongs to my Christian profession, … to be slandered, reproached and reviled; and since all this is nothing else, … I rejoice in reproaches for Christ's sake!'

(A booklet about Agnes Beaumont of Edworth, by Patricia L. Bell, published by The Belfry Press, Bedford, is available from the Bunyan Museum, Bedford)

The final journey

During the summer of 1688 a distressed neighbour in Bedford asked Bunyan to intervene in a dispute he had with his father.

Pictured:
Snow Hill, Holborn,
London today. Bunyan
died here in August
1688

Opposite:
John Bunyan's tomb,
Bunhill Fields, London

Bunyan, more than willing to help, promised to visit the angry father at his home in Reading in Berkshire. He had already planned to set out in the middle of August for a preaching tour into London and decided to go to Reading on the way. Elizabeth was anxious, because her husband had suffered with poor health since the spring that year, and she questioned whether he should undertake such

an arduous journey. However, John insisted.

The meeting with the angry father in Reading was successfully concluded and Bunyan left the town and travelled east towards the capital on the 16th August. Unfortunately the weather gave way to heavy storms and showers. John would have been wise to seek shelter but he pressed on with the journey and arrived at the home of his friend John Strudwick, a grocer in Snow Hill, Holborn, late in the day. He was exhausted, shivering with cold and soaked to the skin; he went to bed immediately with a hot drink of selected herbs. Although unwell the next day he did improve a little and on the following Sunday, 19 August 1688, he was able to preach at the meeting house in Petticoat Lane, Whitechapel. It was a powerful sermon from the text: 'Which were born, not of blood, nor of the will of the flesh, nor of the will of man, but of God' (John 1:13, AV). This was the last sermon he preached.

On the following Tuesday Bunyan developed pneumonia and was confined to bed with a high fever. The doctor that was summoned to see him at Strudwick's home could do very little. It is probable that the friends who cared so lovingly for him over the next ten days were unaware of the critical condition he was in as Elizabeth was not informed or sent for.

On Friday 31 August 1688 a thunderstorm over the metropolis broke the silence of the early hours. It had been a hot, humid summer's night, and several close

JOHN BUNYAN,
AUTHOR OF THE
PILGRIMS PROGRESS
OBT 31ST AUGT 1688,
ÆT 60.

friends including John Strudwick, and Charles Doe of Southwark, had attended Bunyan throughout the night, as death seemed imminent.

The storm passed and the late summer sun filled the dying preacher's bedroom, warming his sallow face. Presently he looked at those around him. They drew closer, asking what could be done for him? 'Brothers' he said, softly, 'I desire nothing more than to be with Christ, which is far better.' He loosened the grip of their friendly grasp, ready as it were to be released from all that bound him to this earth—he lifted his head slightly from the pillow as a slight colour returned to his cheeks and his blue eyes sparkled in the bright sunshine. With arms outstretched, he cried victoriously, 'TAKE ME FOR I COME TO THEE!' John Bunyan died triumphantly. For him, as with Christian in his now famous allegory, the trumpets were to sound on the other side.

John Bunyan was buried on 3 September in Bunhill Fields in the City of London in the family tomb of the Strudwicks. A large number of Puritan acquaintances attended the burial in the graveyard where many well-known dissenters were to be buried over the years, including such names as John Owen, Isaac Watts, Daniel Defoe and Susannah Wesley, the mother of the Methodist preachers, John and Charles. The news of his death reached Bedford on 2 September. It was a sad loss to Elizabeth, who outlived her husband a further four years, and to his surviving children, as well as to his many friends at the church in Mill Lane. An entry in the church minute book records his death. The stress of the occasion is apparent because there is a discrepancy between the day and date '… Wednesday the 4th of September was kept in prayer and humiliation for this heavy stroke upon us, the death of brother Bunyan…' John was greatly missed by his congregation at Bedford and it would be three years before a successor to his pastorate was found.

John Bunyan was undoubtedly one of the Christian 'greats' of the 17th century, a great preacher, a great author and a champion for the struggling nonconformist church. But perhaps the most remarkable legacy of 'the tinker of Elstow' is that here in the 21st century, his writings of free expression and faith are as powerful and real today as when first published during those troubled times in English history.

Left: Wainwood, Hertfordshire. The natural 'amphitheatre' bowl where John Bunyan held secret meetings

TRAVEL INFORMATION

Wain wood

Preston, Hertfordshire

**OS Grid reference
TL 181254**

also:

Coleman Green

**near Wheathampstead.
Hertfordshire. OS Grid
reference TL 190125**

Neither site is suitable for wheelchair access.
From Bedford town centre, drive towards Hitchin on the A600, 29 kilometres (18 miles). In Hitchin, follow A 602 to Stevenage for 1.5 kilometres (1 mile). After passing under a concrete footbridge, at the roundabout take the road to Gosmore. (Driving from Bedford via A1(M) south, leave at Junction 8, follow A602 to Hitchin for 4 kilometres (2.5 miles) then at the first

roundabout take the road to Gosmore. Drive through the village of Gosmore, towards Preston, 4 kilometres (2.5 miles). Park in the centre of Preston at the village green (near the Red Lion Public House). On foot, return a short distance along Hitchin Road (by which you entered the village), turning left into Chequers Lane. After walking a few hundred metres, just before you reach Templars Lane, is a swing gate on the right-hand side in a hedge. Take this footpath to Wain wood across open farmland keeping to the right hand edge of the

field until you reach a gate leading into the wood on the right. Soon after you enter the wood the footpath descends a hill. The natural 'amphitheatre' bowl, (now covered in undergrowth) where John Bunyan held secret meetings, can be seen after walking a short distance on the right-hand side of the footpath. For a circular walk, of approximately 3 kilometres (2 miles), continue along the footpath beyond a cottage (named 'Bunyan's Cottage') until the main road is reached, then turn right for Preston. On the picturesque village green,

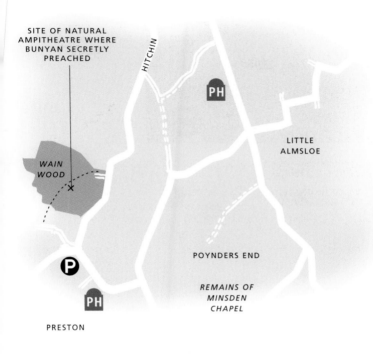

SITE OF NATURAL
AMPITHEATRE WHERE
BUNYAN SECRETLY
PREACHED

HITCHIN

PH

LITTLE
ALMSLOE

*WAIN
WOOD*

POYNDERS END

P

*REMAINS OF
MINSDEN
CHAPEL*

PH

PRESTON

KEY P= Parking   **PH**= Public House   SCALE = 1 MILE

to the right of a distinctive water pump, is Church Lane. A converted chapel, once known as 'Ebenezer', stands beyond in this lane. The stone tablet on the front wall refers to connections with the Bunyan family.

Leave Preston by School Lane in the direction of Whitwell, turning left into St. Albans Highway at first junction after 1 kilometre (1/2 mile). Descending gradually down the hill for 2 kilometres (1 mile) turn right at the junction for Little Almshoe, and drive for 1 kilometre (1/2 mile) to reach the B656 road. Turn right and continue on this road for 8 kilometres (5miles) for Codicote. In the centre of the village turn right into St. Albans Road (just after passing The Bell Public House) in the direction of Wheathampstead. After 9 kilometres (5 miles) turn left at the junction with the B653. Continue along this road crossing the River Lea, turning left towards Welwyn Garden City at the next roundabout. In 1 kilometre (1/2 mile) turn right for Coleman Green, which is reached along a single-track road after 1.5 kilometres (1 mile). At Coleman Green, the remains of the cottage where Bunyan is said to have preached are preserved in a small, hedged enclosure on the left, opposite two small semi-detached brick

KEY 1 Bunyan's tomb 2 Wesley Museum 3 Liverpool Street Station

cottages. The John Bunyan Public House stands off the road opposite a green area. Park off the road using the car park behind the telephone kiosk.

When leaving Coleman Green, return to the B653 and turn right towards Welwyn Garden City. After 3 kilometres (2 miles) turn left into Lemsford (by the village church) and drive through the village. At the far end of Lemsford follow the road directions for A1(M) (Junction 5) to return north to Bedfordshire.

John Bunyan Statue

A statue of John Bunyan can be seen on the Baptist Church House, which is on the east side of Southampton Row, Bloomsbury, London WC1.

Wesley's Chapel and the Museum of Methodism

49 City Road EC1 1AU
☎ 020 7253 2262
www.wesleyschapel.
org.uk

There is an admission charge and disabled access by ramp and lift.

An excellent introduction to the life of John Wesley. The small house in which he lived from 1779 until his death in 1791 is on the same site and can be toured. Many artefacts of Wesley are on show in the house and museum. His tomb is behind the Chapel.

Around Bunhill Fields

Bunhill Fields
City Road EC1

You can freely walk through the cemetery on the main path, but to gain access to the tombs you will need to contact beforehand:
The Parks department on
☎ 020 8472 3584
Fax. 020 8475 0893
email: parks.gardens@
ms.corpoflondon.gov.uk
or call ☎ 020 7247 8548
The nearest tube stations are Old Street (exit 4) on the Northern Line, or Moorgate on the Northern, Circle and Metropolitan lines.

Known as 'The Cemetery of Puritan England', here lie the remains of many evangelical 'greats' of past centuries. After the Restoration of the monarchy in 1660 nonconformists were unable to be buried in church graveyards without a prayer book service. The Public Records Office holds the records of burials here since 1713, though it was in use long before then. It was closed for burial in 1853. A dissenting meeting place stood here in 1666.

Among the many tombs here are those of John Owen (a great theologian and chaplain to Oliver Cromwell), Charles Fleetwood (son in law to Cromwell and one of his generals), the hymn writers Isaac Watts, and Joseph Hart, and Susanna Wesley (the mother of John and Charles Wesley). Immediately opposite the tomb of John Bunyan is the memorial to Daniel Defoe, author of *Robinson Crusoe* and himself an evangelical Christian.

Within one mile of Bunhill

Museum of London
London Wall, EC2Y 5HN
☎ 020 7600 3699
www.museumoflondon.
org.uk

Built into the old city wall and overlooking part of the Roman wall, the museum traces the history of London from the earliest times. Items relating to Christian history are on display in the various departments. Outside the main entrance is the plaque telling of John Wesley's conversion.

Around the City

From the Museum of London you can walk along London Wall and down Moorgate to the heart of the City of London.

St Mary Woolnoth

Lombard Street and King William Street, EC4.

John Newton, the ex slave-trader and sea captain, became rector here from 1780 until his death in 1807. Apart from the removal of his gallery, the church is much as it was in Newton's time, including the massive pulpit and the clock outside the church. There is a marble monument to Newton inside the church. He was buried here but later his remains were removed to his first parish in Olney, Buckinghamshire.

Little Britain

EC1 (almost opposite the London Museum to the south west)

Little Britain: a small street with a big history

A small street with a big history! Three hundred years ago Little Britain was the home of many book-sellers. Famous people lodged here for periods of time: John Milton (1662), Samuel Johnson (at the age of three in 1712), and Benjamin Franklin (1724). Of especial interest is the blue and gold plaque over a doorway that commemorates the site where Charles Wesley was converted in 1738 just three days before his brother John.

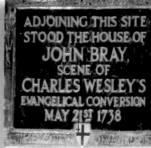

ADJOINING THIS SITE STOOD THE HOUSE OF **JOHN BRAY**, SCENE OF CHARLES WESLEY'S EVANGELICAL CONVERSION MAY 21ST 1738

Smithfield

EC1 (at the top of Little Britain)

Once a 'smooth field' just outside the City wall it was a popular place for tournaments and jousting seven hundred years ago. Wat Tyler and his rebels confronted Richard II here in 1381 and for four hundred years it became a notorious place for the execution of criminals. During the reign of Queen Mary 200 'heretics' were burned to death here—many of them evangelical reformers. Note the railings that commemorate these events, painted black with gold tops to mimic flames.

By 1638 the area had been paved and a cattle market was established; the market stayed here until 1855 from which year only dead meat was sold.

Christchurch

Newgate Street, EC1
(opposite Warwick Lane)

The gardens mark the site of a thirteenth century Franciscan monastery that was converted into a church (Christchurch) in 1547. It was rebuilt by Sir Christopher Wren after the Great Fire of 1666. Buried here are Isobella, the wife of Edward II and their daughter, Joan, Queen of Scotland. Richard Baxter, the Puritan preacher and minister at Kidderminster is also buried here. Richard Neville, Earl of Warwick, known as the King-maker because he helped to establish first Edward IV and then Henry VI during the Wars of the Roses, lived in Warwick Lane in 1450.

St Dunstan in the West

Fleet Street, EC4

This old church escaped the Fire of London. The original building was demolished in 1830 and this one was erected. The eight bells are from the original building, as is the famous clock (1671), said to be the first in London to have the face marked in minutes. The poet John Donne was rector here from 1621 until his death in 1631; his bust is on the east side of the porch. The church witnessed the preaching of some great evangelical men. William Tyndale, the Reformer who gave us the first English New Testament translated from the Greek and printed (1526) came to London in 1523 and preached here. There is a bust of Tyndale on the west side of the porch. From 1749 to 1766 William Romaine, the godly evangelical minister, was granted permission to preach here and his sermons packed the church with an attentive congregation.

London Guildhall

Gresham Street, EC2
☎ 020 7606 3030
www.cityoflondon.gov.uk
Free entry

Rebuilt after the Great Fire of 1666, Guildhall hosts many state occasions, and encloses some of the original medieval buildings. In the great hall is a list of famous trials that were held here, including Anne Askew, Lady Jane Grey and her husband Lord Guildford Dudley, and

conversion attended evensong in the Cathedral. Outside the main entrance stood the Lollards tower where many protestants were imprisoned. St Paul's Churchyard was once a place for the execution of martyrs and it was a centre for the London book trade. It was here that the bishop of London (Tunstall) publicly burned William Tyndale's Bibles in the 1520s and 30s.

The Barbican Centre
Silk Street
☎ Box office:
020 7638 8891
www.barbican.org.uk
Nearest tube: Barbican, on the Circle, Metropolitan and Hammersmith & City lines. Exit the station and cross Aldersgate Street in front. Walk through the road tunnel (Beech Street) and take the first turning right into Silk Street. The Centre is then straight ahead.

It is Europe's largest multi-arts and conference venue, presenting a year-round programme of art, music, film and theatre. It has two theatres, two cinemas and is the London home of the Royal Shakespeare Company. It also has plenty of places to eat, catering for different tastes.

Archbishop Thomas Cranmer. It is a microcosm of the City's history.

St Paul's Cathedral

**St Paul's Churchyard
EC4**
☎ 020 7236 4128
www.stpauls.co.uk
Admission charge

This is the fourth cathedral built on this site of a Roman temple to the goddess Diana. The cathedral was rebuilt by Sir Christopher Wren after the Great Fire of 1666. The cross surmounting the famous dome is 365 feet above the ground. It took 35 years to build and Wren visited the site every week. He is buried in the crypt. Lord Nelson (the Battle of Trafalgar in 1805) and the Duke of Wellington (Waterloo in 1815) are among many famous people buried here. Sir Winston Churchill's funeral was held here, as was the wedding of Prince Charles and Princess Diana. If you are fit a walk up to the whispering gallery is a must, then up to the outside galleries for views of London.

In the garden is a fine statue of John Wesley, who on the day of his

BEDFORDSHIRE

Bedfordshire local information and selected Eating Guide

**Bedford Tourist
Information Centre**
10 St. Paul's Square
Bedford MK40 1SL
☎ 01234 215226
Fax: 01234 217932
email: tic@Bedford.gov.uk

Ampthill Visitor Centre
Mid Beds District Council
The Limes
Dunstable Street
Ampthill Beds MK45 2JU
☎ 01525 402051

**Woburn Heritage
Centre**
Old St. Mary's Church
Bedford Street
Woburn, Beds
MK17 9PJ
☎ 01525 290631

**Sandy Tourist
Information Centre**
A1 Sandy Roundabout
Girtford Bridge.
5 Shannon Court, High St,
Sandy Beds SG19 1AG
☎ 01767 682728

Online information

**http://www.bedford.
gov.uk**
The official web site of
Bedford Borough Council.
http://www.bedford
shire.gov.uk
The official web site of
Bedfordshire County
Council.
http://www.beds.co.uk
A local Bedford web site
with useful information
about Bedford and the
surrounding area.

PLACES OF INTEREST

Woburn Safari Park

Woburn, Bedfordshire
☎ 01525 290407

**OS map reference
SP345967**

Set in a part of the
Woburn estate, the
seat of the Duke of
Bedford, the safari park is
in three hundred acres of
open parkland. The safari
drive experience takes you
through open reserves of
animals including wolves,
bears, tigers, and lions.

There is also a monkey enclosure, pet's corner and a walk-through aviary.

Open March-October 10am-5pm. Weekends only in winter 11am–3pm.

Woburn Abbey

Woburn, Bedfordshire

☎ 01525 290666
www.woburnabbey.co.uk

OS Map reference SP333975

Woburn Abbey has been the home of the Russell Family, the Dukes of Bedford for over 450 years. The house is an 18th century palatial mansion surrounded by a three thousand acre deer park. The tour of the abbey covers three floors, including Queen Victoria's bedroom. The treasures are renowned among the finest private collections in England, with paintings by Joshua Reynolds, Canaletto and Gainsborough. Open daily March—Sept Weekends only Nov—Dec.

The Swiss Gardens

**Old Warden,
Nr Biggleswade**

☎ 01767 627666
www.shuttleworth.
org/swissgardens

OS Map reference TL148448

Part of the Shuttleworth estate, this unique 19th century ornamental Swiss Garden is reportedly one of the top ten gardens in the country. Landscaped with a network of paths that meander through avenues of rare trees and shrubs, around ponds with islands and decorative iron bridges. The garden contains a number of follies and a variety of miniature buildings and other garden structures.

The Shuttleworth Collection

**Old Warden,
Nr Biggleswade**

☎ 01767 627288
www.shuttleworth.org

OS Map reference TL151448

A famous collection of aircraft, cars and carriages displayed in seven hangars in the traditional setting of a 1930s grass aerodrome. The collection, started by Richard Shuttleworth, traces the birth of flight through to Second World War aircraft. Summer flying displays are a popular event–for details and times call
☎ 09068 323310 (Calls cost 60p per minute).

The Forest of Marston Vale

☎ 01234 767037
www.marstonvale.org

OS Map reference
TL005415

The forest in Mid-Bedfordshire is one of many new forests to be funded recently by the British government and received over £5m from the Millennium

Commission and partners. Over one hundred and fifty hectares of trees, shrubs and flowers have already been planted around seventeen villages. At the Forest Visitor Centre, set in the Millennium Country Park at Marston Moretaine, are cycleways, bridlepaths, rare wetland habitats for wild birds and wildlife as well as wildlife displays, an interactive exhibition and café. Admission to the Millennium Park and Forest Centre is free.

Willington Dovecote and Stables

www.nationaltrust.org.uk
OS Map reference
TL107500

A 16th century stable and stone dovecote, built by John Gostwick, Cardinal Wolsey's Master of the Horse. The unique dovecote is lined with 1500 nesting boxes for pigeons. The stable block of buff-grey stone, which stands nearby, and once known as 'King Henry's Stable', has an upper floor with finely moulded windows. Above the large stone fireplace is an inscription 'JOHN BVNYAN 1650' which he chiselled whilst working as a tinker. The two buildings are now under the ownership of the National Trust. The keys are available by appointment with Mrs J Endersby, 21 Chapel Lane, Willington, Bedford MK44 3QG ☎ 01234 838278 Admission charge £1 (Not suitable for wheelchair access).

Willington is 8 kilometres (5 miles) east of Bedford on the A603 road towards Sandy. The Dovecote is clearly signposted.

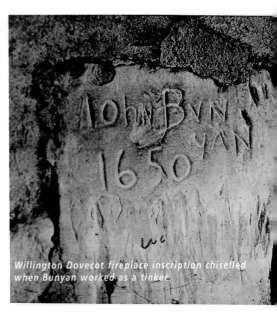

Willington Dovecot fireplace inscription chiselled when Bunyan worked as a tinker

The John Bunyan Trail

The Ramblers Association (Bedfordshire Area) has created a trail throughout Bedfordshire dedicated to John Bunyan to mark their sixtieth Jubilee. Known as the John Bunyan Trail, it takes walkers through places connected with Bunyan, as well as secret meetings sites, and those that are associated with places mentioned in *The Pilgrim's Progress*.

The trail is clearly marked on local Ordinance Survey 'Landranger' Maps and further details of the trail, which is in two sections, are available from local Tourist Information Centres.

Mid Bedfordshire Scenic Route

An eighty-mile road trail that winds through the lovely countryside and villages of Bedfordshire, some of which have connections with John Bunyan. The route, which is clearly marked by brown directional road signs, passes beautiful landscapes and visits interesting places, many steeped in history. Details available from local Information Centres.

EATING OUT

A food and drink guide for Bedford and Mid Bedfordshire is available from local tourist information centres. Details given include suggestions for traditional country pubs and inns, bistros, restaurants and take-away bars.

Selected Restaurants in Bedford

Saffron Restaurant
(Indian)
64 Tavistock Street,
MK40 2RG
☎ **01234 324655**
(Clean and modern)

Debenhams
46 High Street
MK40 1ST
☎ **01234 342581**
(Open during shopping hours only. Serves a range of hot & cold meals)

Gulshan Restaurant
(Indian)
69-71 Tavistock Street,
MK40 2RR
☎ 01234 355544

KFC
63 Tavistock Street
MK40 2RR
(Eat in or take-away)

McDonalds Restaurant
9 High Street, MK40 1RN
☎ 01234 360544
(Eat in or take-away)

Indiya Restaurant
1-2 The Broadway,
MK40 2TE
☎ 01234 327493
(Opposite Bunyan's statue)

The Sizzling Wok
(Mongolian)
3 The Broadway, MK40 2TJ
☎ 01234 212888

Pizzeria Santaniello
9 Newnham Street,
MK40 3JR
01234 353742
(Authentic Italian dishes)

Chef Beijing (Chinese)
52-54 Castle Lane, (Ram Yard), MK40 3NU
☎ 01234 273883

Nicholls Brasserie
38 The Embankment,
MK40 3PF
☎ 01234 212848
(Good cuisine with views of the river)

Above: The garden of St Helena Restaurant is the site of Bunyan's cottage

Paprika (Indian)
36 The Broadway, MK40
☎ 01234 355944
(Bedford's first non-smoking restaurant)

Pizza Hut
68 High St,
MK40
(Near the site
of the Old
Bedford Gaol)
☎ 01234 271 575

Caffe Crema
59 High Street, MK40 1RZ
☎ 01234 330518
(Italian Coffee House)

Bounders
99 High Street, MK40 1NE
☎ 01234 266912
(Breakfasts, Brunches & Baguettes)

The Piazza
St Pauls Square, Bedford
MK40 1SQ
☎ 01234 328433
(For open-air snacks)

The Swan Hotel
The Embankment, Bedford
☎ 01234 346565
(Restaurant overlooks the river)

See picture below

**Elstow
Village
Restaurants**

Brewers Fayre (pub)
Red Lion, High Street
Elstow
MK42 9XP
☎ 01234 359687
(Caters for all the family)

St Helena Restaurant
High Street Elstow,
MK42 9XP
☎ 01234 344848
(High class, country house restaurant. Advance booking essential)
See top picture

TRAVEL NOTES

Useful information

You may be a very experienced traveller who has learned all the tips to make for a pleasant day of touring. The following notes are for those who are new to visiting places of interests, and especially for overseas visitors; a little information about your host country will make you feel more at home and less of a stranger. Travelling around in the UK is easy if a few things are remembered.

1 What do you wear?

Wear comfortable clothes and shoes. Travelling on public transport can be hot and dirty; so it is better to dress comfortably than smartly. Wear thin layers (relevant to the season) topped with a light waterproof coat that can protect from wind as well as rain. It is easier to carry two or more thinner garments than a heavy coat and jumper if the weather changes from cold to fine. Remember that the only reliable thing about the British weather is that it is unreliable!

2 Take great care with personal belongings.

Keep wallets and purses out of sight, on your person, as bags can easily be snatched. Cameras and other personal items should be kept secure at all times. A rucksack may be good for your back, but be careful on crowded public transport or in bustling city streets, it can be opened and items removed without your knowledge. Never put a bag down and walk off, it will probably have disappeared when you return—it may have been stolen or possibly blown up as a suspected bomb! All this is especially ímportant in our cities and towns, but don't assume that your property is more secure just because you are in the heart of rural Britain. Being aware of possible problems will enable you to enjoy your sightseeing. Normally when precautions are taken an incident will not arise. And rest easy—Britain is still one of the safest countries in the world to travel around in, and the evidence of this is that our police do not carry guns.

3 For overseas visitors.

Do not carry your passport with you, unless you plan to change money. Most hotels have a safe where you can store valuable items. If you think you may need your passport for identification often a photocopy will do. In fact it is a good idea to take a photocopy of the relevant pages of your passport and carry this with you always, separate from the original passport. If the original is lost then it will be easier for your embassy to issue a temporary document from the information on the photocopy.

4 Obtain a map of public transport in the area you are travelling. Basic maps are free from tourist information kiosks; bus and railway maps are available from bus garages (depots/terminus) and major railway stations. If a particular site mentioned in this book is on the mainline railway network then the

station is referred to and instructions of the best way to get to it are given.

5 Always respect the places you visit.

Take note of 'No Entry' and 'Private' signs. A private dwelling may once have had a connection with the subject of this book, but the present residents may consider it an intrusion if you disturb them. We have tried to indicate where access is or is not permitted. Usually there will be an indication at the property if it is open for public viewing.

6 Photography. Respect any 'No Photographs permitted' signs,

and if a fee is requested to take photographs then it must be paid. In some museums and historic buildings you may take photographs, but you are not permitted to use a tripod since this can be very annoying to other visitors. Please bear this in mind when deciding on the speed of film you buy. The general rule should be never to use a camera in museums and historic buildings without enquiring first. A polite enquiry can save hassle. Take enough film for the day. You

are well advised not to buy film from a street vendor, however cheap they may appear; old or poor quality film can ruin your valuable memories. Always buy in a reputable shop, and get a receipt in case the film is faulty. Look for the 'three for the price of two' offers during the peak season.

7 In a museum, exhibition or church,

do not touch anything that you are not permitted to

handle. Not only can an object be damaged, but also in certain circumstances prosecution may result because of your action, however unintended it may have been.

8 Respect graves. In a cemetery, church or

churchyard, please be careful where you tread, especially if a service is taking place. A good rule of thumb is to consider how you would feel if someone came and disturbed the resting-place of your loved ones. You may want to stand on a tomb or grave to get a good

photograph, but remember that this could cause offence. Walk around a church or graveyard without raising your voice; someone may be sitting quietly by the grave of their loved one.

9 When walking in the countryside, please

respect the country code. Leave gates as you found them—whether open or closed. Keep to the paths, or walk around the edge of fields. Please do not drop litter—farm animals are not very smart and will chew on your discarded plastic bags and take-away dishes, often with tragic results. Animals should be left in peace, and if you have a dog with you, make sure that it does not worry any livestock. Be very careful not to start a fire, especially in hot dry weather.

10 Litter. Please be careful with the

disposal of all litter. In many cities it will not be easy to find litter bins due to terrorist activities. Therefore you may have to take your rubbish back home with you. Chewing Gum. If you use gum please be careful in the

disposal of it after use, some places are considering bringing in heavy fines to deter thoughtless discarding of it; and reference libraries will ask you to remove it from your mouth if they see you chewing!

11 You will probably find it useful to put together a tourist pack. We suggest the following: a notebook, a pen or pencil, a small torch with batteries that work and a small medical kit. These things will not take up a lot of room but may be useful to you at some stage.

12 Eating out. For most trips you may prefer to prepare a packed lunch. This can save time looking around for suitable food outlets. Remember that city eating places can be expensive. If a hot meal is required there are many different types of food outlets to suit all tastes and styles. Many Garden Centres have excellent cafeterias or restaurants and are usually good value for money. These are normally open for food

between 10.00am and 4.00pm. Good rural public houses (pubs) can also provide quality service.

13 Disabled visitors All public buildings in the UK are under a legal requirement to be wheelchair accessible; those in charge of such places are usually very helpful, but in old buildings full access is not always possible. We have indicated where access may be difficult or where there may be particular problems, or special facilities, for the disabled, visually impaired or the hard of hearing. Please let us know if you discover things that have deteriorated—or improved.

14 Public conveniences (restrooms) In cities these are usually open until about 6pm. Most major stores,

large petrol stations and **every** restaurant or café will have conveniences. As a last resort if it is late or you are in a small village, there is usually one in a public house. Some landlords will not be happy for you to just walk in to use the convenience, if in doubt buy a snack (crisps or nuts etc.) this usually pacifies them. Always carry tissues (Kleenex) with you, as some public conveniences will not have any toilet tissue; better to be safe than sorry.

15 Especially for London A London combined network map (bus, underground and overground railways) is available from bus garages, underground stations, overland railway stations and also many newsagents who display the London transport

sign.
Travel to all London sites will be referred to from one of the main London termini. If you are staying on the outskirts of London or travelling in for the day from another location, note beforehand where you need to be and how long it will take you to get there, a little planning can save wasted time (see page 128).

The best time to travel around London on a weekday is after 9.30am. You can save a lot of money if your train leaves after this time, and you avoid the rush hour. The transport companies have divided London into zones, and the number of zones visited will determine the cost of the ticket. The best ticket to buy is a Travel Card (you can get daily, weekly or monthly cards). Travel Cards will enable the user to go by overland train, tube and bus all on the same ticket. Make sure that you buy the right ticket for the places to be visited; just ask the clerk in the ticket office, they will tell you the best ticket for your needs.

Refreshments in London are many and various. It would be best to have a packed lunch as we suggest above, but if you prefer hot food, please take note of the following: Always check that the food and drink prices are listed before you place an order; this way you will not end up paying unnecessarily high prices. If it appears that you are a foreigner, or from out of town it is not unknown for extras to suddenly appear on a bill (check). Always query any discrepancies before payment is made. Drinks and food from road-side vendors in the cities will be more expensive.

Unless you have a good budget, the best places for light refreshments are fast food restaurants, especially if you just want a hot drink. Another possibility worth investigating is any café that builders are using! They may not be the most luxurious surroundings, but the workers normally know where to find good wholesome food, that is served quickly and hot—and at a reasonable price. You will also gain an interesting insight into London life!

Finally—well, nearly!

These basic guidelines are not meant to hinder but enhance your enjoyment as you travel around.
If on your travels you come across other sights or places of related interest not mentioned in this book, would you kindly let the publisher know, and any future edition may be able to include this information for the enjoyment of other travellers.

Enjoy your journey!

Useful Telephone Numbers

In an emergency call ☎ **999** and ask for Fire, Police or Ambulance.
Remember to tell the operator, **Where the trouble is, What the trouble is, Where you are.** Also give the number of the phone you are using. Never make a false call, you could risk the lives of others that really need help and it is against the law. You can also be traced immediately to the phone where the call came from.

If you need help in making a call that is Local or National, call free on ☎ **100**. If help is required in making an International call, call free on ☎ **155**.

If you require help in finding a number or code call Directory Enquiries, you will be charged for this service. For Local and national numbers call ☎ **192**. International numbers call ☎ **153**.

Travelodge reservations:
☎ 08700 850 950.
www.travelodge.co.uk

Travel Inn reservations:
☎ 0870 242 8000.

Tourist Information Centres:
www.mistral.co.uk/hammerwood/uk.htm

National Rail enquiries:
☎ 0845 7 48 49 50. Or for the hard of hearing, 0845 60 50 600. www.rail.co.uk

London Transport:
☎ 020 7222 1234
www.londontransport.co.uk/London Transport
www.londontransport.co.uk/

DATE	AGE	EVENT
Autumn 1628	Birth	Born at Harrowden in the parish of Elstow, Bedfordshire.
Spring 1644	16	Margaret, John's mother, dies. John's sister Margaret died within a month. Both were buried in Elstow churchyard.
		Two months after his wife's death, Thomas Bunyan, John's father, marries his third wife.
1645	16	Enters army—Comrade killed in his place.
1647	19	Returns home and resumes work in the family business as a tinker.
1649	21	Marries first wife. (Name unknown)
20 July 1650	22	Mary, his much-loved blind daughter and eldest child, is christened at Elstow.
1653	25	Vision on Elstow Green whilst playing tip-cat (date uncertain).
		Enters a period of spiritual turmoil. Commences to attend St John's church in Bedford, where he meets John Gifford, the pastor.
1653?		Baptised in Bedford River
14 April 1654	26	Mary's younger sister, Elizabeth, is christened at Elstow.
1655	27	Moves to a cottage in St. Cuthbert's Street Bedford. John Gifford dies in September of the same year.
1656	28	Bunyan appointed to preach in public by the church at St. John's. Publishes first work entitled *Some Gospel Truths Opened*.
1657	29	Publishes second work entitled *Vindication of Gospel Truths*.
		Appointed as a deacon of the church.
1658	30	Indictment is laid against John at the Assizes for 'preaching at Eaton Socon'. The charge was most likely dropped.
1659	31	Publishes third work led entitled *A Few Sighs From Hell*. Marries his second wife, Elizabeth. Publishes *The Doctrine of the Law and Grace Unfolded*. The last book he writes before being placed in prison.
12 Nov 1660	32	Arrested at the hamlet of Lower Samsell near Harlington.
		Placed in Bedford prison and charged with 'devilishly and perniciously abstaining from coming to church to hear divine service'.
November 1660	32	Approximately eight days after John's arrest, his wife gives birth to a stillborn child
August 1661	33	John's wife goes before the judges, to ask that her husband's case be considered. She is denied.
1663	35	Publishes *A Discourse Touching Prayer*. Writes *Christian Behaviour*.
1664	36	Publishes *One Thing Is Needful* on single sheets to be sold by his wife and children, to aid them financially.

DATE	AGE	EVENT
1665	37	Writes *The Holy City* and *The Resurrection of the Dead and Eternal Judgment* from Bedford prison. Writes a poem entitled *Prison Meditations* in response to a letter he received, exhorting him to hold his head above the flood.
1666	38	Publishes *Grace Abounding to the Chief of Sinners*.
1671	43	Released from Bedford prison, after twelve years of imprisonment.
		Appointed Pastor of the Bedford Independent church.
1674	46	Publishes *Christian Behaviour* as a pocket volume.
1675	47	Writes *The Pilgrim's Progress* during six months of further incarceration.
		After being released the same year, he resumes his pastorate.
1676	48	Publishes *The Strait Gate*.
February 1678	50	Publishes *The Pilgrim's Progress*.
1678	50?	Second edition of *The Pilgrim's Progress* is published in the autumn.
1679	51	Publishes *A Treatise of the Fear of God*.
1680	52	Publishes *The Life and Death of Mr. Badman*.
1681	53	Publishes, *Come and Welcome to Jesus Christ*.
1682	54	Publishes *The Holy War*. Publishes the eighth edition of *The Pilgrim's Progress*, and makes last improvements.
1684	56	Publishes ninth edition of *The Pilgrim's Progress*. Publishes the second part of *The Pilgrim's Progress* and *Seasonable Counsel*.
1685	57	Publishes tenth edition of *The Pilgrim's Progress*. In danger of returning to prison.
1688	60	Publishes *The Water of Life*.
1688	60	Publishes *The Jerusalem Sinner Saved* in a pocket volume of eight sheets.
August 1688	60	Preaches his last sermon on 19th August from John 1:13. Dies at the end of the month. *The Barren Fig Tree* is reprinted a few months after John's decease.
1689	-	*The Acceptable Sacrifice* is published. The manuscript found in his pocket at the time of his death.
1691	-	*The Jerusalem Sinner Saved* is reprinted.
		Charles Doe publishes *An Exposition on the First Ten Chapters of Genesis, and Part of the Eleventh*, found among John Bunyan's papers after his death, in his own handwriting.
1692	-	Elizabeth Bunyan, John's second wife, dies.
1698	-	Charles Doe publishes *The Heavenly Footman*.
1701	-	*A Book For Boys and Girls* is first published.

126

BIBLIOGRAPHY

Bacon, E. 1983 *Pilgrim and Dreamer* The Paternoster Press, Exeter.

Britten, V. 1950 *In the steps of John Bunyan* Rich and Cowan, London (Reprinted 1970).

Evans, V. 1988 *John Bunyan His life and Times* The Book Castle, Dunstable.

Godber, J. 1969 *History of Bedfordshire* Bedfordshire County Council.

Hart, M. 2000 *Portrait of Elstow* C&C Printers, Bedford

Hinde, T. 1997 *The Doomsday Book, England's Heritage Now & Then* Bramley Books, Godalming, Surrey.

Lupton L. 1975 *Behind Mr Bunyan,* The Fauconberg Press, London

Mott Harrison, F. 1928 *John Bunyan A story of his life* Banner of Truth, Edinburgh.

Smith, A. 1998 *The British Particular Baptists Vol. 1* Particular Baptist Press, Springfield Missouri.

Stanley, A. 1947 *The Bedside Bunyan* Eyre and Spottiswoode, London.

The standard biography of Bunyan is *John Bunyan: His Life, Times and Work*, by **Rev. J Brown BA, DD.** Minister of Bunyan Meeting, Bedford, 1864-1903. **Frank Mott Harrison** revised the work in 1928.

ACKNOWLEDGMENTS

Malcolm P Carvell for factual and detail advice

Charlotte Gabrielle Deamer for her invaluable help with the photography

John Dunn (Australia) Biographical notes and references

Canon Richard Huband for information relating to Elstow Parish Church

Nigel Lutt Bedfordshire County Records and Archive Service

Doreen Watson and the Trustees of Bunyan Meeting Free Church Bedford

Rosemary Pestell for patience and inspiration

Paul Sayer for his help with the maps

Terry Waite in prison

When the peace envoy, Terry Waite languished in solitary confinement at the hands of his kidnappers in Beirut, he received a simple picture postcard from England which revived his hope. On his release in November 1991, after four years in captivity, he spoke of the way that the good will message together with the image of John Bunyan writing *The Pilgrim's Progress* lifted his spirits and gave him fresh hope.

Notes about the author

John Pestell has been intrigued and closely involved in John Bunyan's life and times throughout his life and, until he married, lived in the main village street at Elstow opposite the site of Bunyan's cottage. Today he still resides in a nearby Bedfordshire village.

When he was born in the mid 1950s, his parents actually lived in Bunyan's cottage. They moved in 1957 and the cottage was demolished in September 1968 for road widening; the author remembers the sense of loss of a historic landmark—and a family home.

John Pestell was educated at the local secondary school, Elstow Abbey, built mid-way between Elstow and Bunyan's birthplace at Harrowden, on the swampy site depicted by Bunyan as the 'Slough of Despond'. John remembers the day when a short cut was sought whilst cross-country running, which brought near disaster as a thirteen-year-old 'athlete' ended up chest deep in quicksands! These were the remains of the marshes that John Bunyan knew so well, but today they are swallowed up by the urban expansion of Bedford.

School day memories remain of looking out through upper storey classroom windows across the fields to Harrowden, and towards the spot where a stone marks the site of Bunyan's birthplace. In the other direction was Elstow village, with its unusual church and separate bell tower and the adjacent Moot Hall on the village green surrounded by quaint old cottages that Bunyan would still recognise today.

Then there are the memories of ball games with school friends on that same village green where Bunyan famously played tip-cat on a particular Sunday afternoon and heard a voice from heaven speaking directly to him. The writer recalls fishing for minnows in the brook near the site of the stepping-stones that Bunyan's family used to cross regularly on the way to Elstow church.

We live in times of religious freedom and tolerance, unlike the middle years of the 17th century in England. John Bunyan is remembered for the way he stood against the established church during

those stormy days even to the point of imprisonment. However, many of the biblical truths he believed, preached and wrote so eloquently about are largely forgotten, over-looked and even denied by so many. John Bunyan's love and knowledge of the Scriptures, the holy word of God, are not widely acknowledged or realised today.

It is hoped that the publication of this book will encourage visitors from home and abroad to find and appreciate the reality of sites and scenes that can still be visited to this day and which will always hold an affinity to Bedfordshire's greatest writer and preacher, John Bunyan. ■

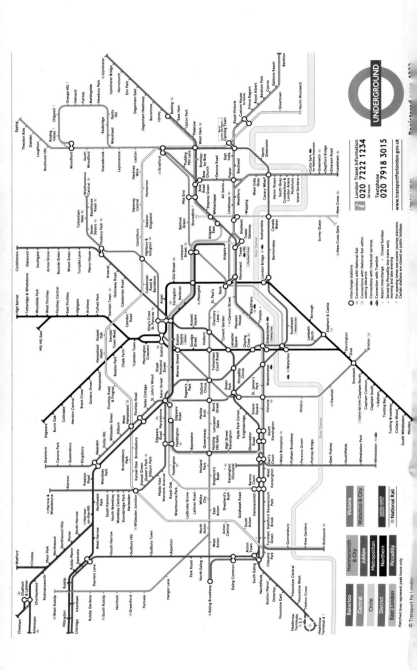

UNDERGROUND

London Travel Information
020 7222 1234
24 hours

Textphone
020 7918 3015
www.transportforlondon.gov.uk

○ Interchange stations
⊖ Connections with National Rail
⊟ Connections with National Rail within walking distance
⋈ Connections with riverboat services
✈ Airport interchange   ● Closed Sundays
△ Served by Piccadilly line trains early morning and late evening
▫ Connection with Tramlink
* For opening times see poster journey planners. Certain stations are closed on public holidays.

Bakerloo
Central
Circle
District
East London

Hammersmith & City
Jubilee
Metropolitan
Northern
Piccadilly

Victoria
Waterloo & City
DLR DLR
≠ National Rail

Hatched lines represent peak hours only

© Transport for London

Registered user No. 02/3682/P